Foreword

Welcome to the first volume of "Wirral Memories" in which we recall Wirral Champion readers' memories and reminiscences of the Wirral of yesteryear.

"Wirral Memories" covers a wide range of subjects over a very long period of time. Not only readers' direct living memories but also reminiscences and stories passed down through generations, together with interesting aspects of local history, both factual and 'mythical'. It also includes poetry and readers' letters.

If you have any interesting memories, recollections or stories of Wirral and its people please send them to;

Wirral Memories, 720 Borough Road, Prenton, Wirral, L42 9JE.

We will do our very best to include them in the next volume of Memories.

In the meantime – good reading!

John M. Birtwistle
Editor/Publisher

The publisher would like to thank all the contributors whose work is included in this book: Muriel Bader, Harold Beckett, Judith Edwards, Cyrus Ferguson, George Heymans, Richard Hutson, Tony Jones, John Lindsey, Michelle McWilliams, Win Moreland, Barbara Nuttall, Gordon Ratcliff, Denis Rose, Karen Ward, Ursula Wilde, Wilf Wilson, Jo Wood, and also Les Cowle, Len Harrow, Sid Lindsay and Fred Thornton for their photographs and illustrations, and particularly Ian and Marilyn Boumphrey for the use of their extensive photographic library and illustrations from their "Yesterday's Wirral" series of books.

The Publisher would also like to thank the businesses and organisations whose generous sponsorship has made this book possible: Alouette Wines, Prenton; Birkenhead School, Oxton; Goulds, West Kirby & Heswall and Kingsmead School, Hoylake.

Wirral Memories Volume 1

ISBN 0-9532991-0-4

First Published in 1998 by
Wirral Champion,
720 Borough Road, Prenton, Wirral

Designed &
Produced by

nemo
0151 709 6789

Contents

Magic Moments

by
Barbara Nuttall

The Magic of a baby's smile,

A lovely hug and kiss,

The Magic of two lovers

On a Springtime walk of bliss,

The Magic of a letter

That comes from distant lands,

The Magic of a surgeon

Who can heal with expert hands,

There are many Magic Moments

That slip away so fast,

But Memories are Magic too,

For they can make them last.

The Baron Boys

by Judith Edwards

The first employee to serve 50 years at Levers, Mr Edwin Baron

THESE days when redundancy is common and few people spend their whole working lives in one company, Bebington pensioner, Ronald Baron, can look back with pride at his father who made employment history.

For Mr Edwin Baron was the first employee to complete 50 years service with Lever Brothers in the early years of the now multi-national company.

Edwin, an engineer, celebrated half a century in soapmaking back in 1936. He was 62 at the time and in honour of the event he was presented with a cheque for £50 and was given a month's holiday with full pay.

His proud son, Ronald, now aged 82, who also worked at Levers as a printer, said their lives revolved around the company, during work hours and outside.

His father was a cornet player and was conductor of the Port Sunlight Silver Prize Band.

Ronald and his brother were both musicians. Ronald played the trumpet and had his own dance band, the Moderniques, playing at Hulme Hall and other local dance halls.

Ronald left Levers to go into business but is still fascinated by his father's achievements and his stories of long ago. Happily he has a record of some of his father's memories of that time captured when he celebrated 50 years at Levers.

Edwin Baron wrote, *"I was twelve years old when I started as an office boy in the advertising department, and that was a busy place in those early days at Warrington. We worked from 6am to 5.30pm.*

"Afterwards I went to the soap

The special bandstand built by Mr Lever, for the Silver Prize Band, for one of its many performances at Thornton Manor.

stamping department which was housed in a large modern building and had ten stamping machines, with six boys to each.

"Then I was apprenticed with my respected father in the engineering department, where I was to spend the rest of my long service with the company. When my father and I came to Port Sunlight we had difficulty finding lodgings.

"We managed to get fixed up in a large house where 21 of us lived. I nearly caused a riot by practising my scales on the cornet on Sunday mornings when the rest of the people were trying to sleep.

"Later my father rented a house in Trafalgar Drive, which at the time was surrounded by muddy fields. There were no proper roads and no lights. Indeed, my first impression of Port Sunlight in 1888 was of mud, fields and still more mud, an unbelievable contrast with the lovely village of today.

"My mother, when she saw the district, asked, 'What sort of a place is this you've brought me to? I shan't live here long.' But in the meantime new houses were already being built and we moved into one of them.

"We joined the congregation which worshipped in a little Wesleyan chapel in Bromborough Road. I entered the choir and am still a member after 48 years. As the district grew the chapel was too small and a school chapel was built. Our late beloved chief, Mr Lever, presented the trustees with a splendid two-manual pedal reed organ. About eight years ago (1932) a fine church was built next to the school chapel and our present Governor, Lord Leverhulme, laid the foundation stone.

"Mr Lever used to come to the factory every day arriving punctually at 8am and he had personal contact with all his staff. When the Sunlight Band

was formed he presented us with a set of instruments.

"Christmas was drawing near and our bandmaster, the late Mr Seddon, having taught us to play some carols, we thought it would be nice to give Mr Lever a surprise by performing outside his home at Thornton Manor.

"But it was such a bitterly cold night that our valves were frozen and we made so much noise blowing into our instruments to thaw them out that Mr Lever heard us and came out before we could get started. This was the forerunner of many pleasant visits paid at Christmas time to the Manor."

Ronald explained that there was a censored version of later events. "My father told me they used to go round the big houses playing carols and were given drinks at every house. The last house was Thornton Manor so you can imagine what condition they were in. On one occasion one of the bandsmen had to be wheeled home in a barrow."

Remembering more formal occasions Edwin wrote, *"I well remember the opening of the Gladstone Hall by the Rt. Hon. W. E. Gladstone MP, in 1891. The newly formed brass band had rehearsed diligently for this event and our rendering of 'A fine old English gentleman' was one of the tit-bits of the day. Our first uniform was a tasselled cap, worn with our ordinary clothes. But when we got full uniform we were a real sensation. Since those days the band has rendered yeoman service in the village and district.*

The Port Sunlight Silver Prize Band. The conductor, Mr Edwin Baron pictured front row 2nd from left.

"Through Lever Brothers kindness we were privileged to enjoy some wonderful trips. On our visit to Paris for the 1900 Exhibition – some 1600 'Sunlighters' went and it was regarded at that time as 'the biggest picnic on record'.

"When we were taken to the Liege Exhibition in 1905 a dinner was given, during which the Belgian band kept playing our national anthem, so that most of the time was spent standing up and sitting down again!

"During the works excursion to Brussels in 1910 I had the honour to be chosen as one of a deputation to wait upon the late King Albert, and he both surprised and pleased us all by telling us that he visited our factory at Port Sunlight incognito some years before coming to the throne. It had been kept so quiet even Mr Lever did not know about it.

"Two red-letter days in the life of the village were, first when Mr Lever was victorious in the elections (In the 1906 General Election he was elected for the Wirral division of Chester, which had never previously returned a liberal). The second was when the honour of a baronetcy was conferred upon him by the late King George. We all crowded into the Auditorium and enthusiasm and excitement were at fever pitch.

"I also have vivid recollections of the first big fire at the works one Sunday night. The blaze could be seen for miles and crowds came from far and wide. I have cause to remember too, the resin fires, when practically all the workmen were recruited to

Above: The first school was in Park Road and is now called the Lyceum — and gradually the village grew!

assist the brigades. The whole district was temporarily blacked out with thick choking smoke."

Writing back in 1936 Mr Baron recalled, *"As I look back over the years I remember how, whenever we wanted to go to Liverpool or Birkenhead, we had to walk to New Ferry, and there were no decent roads, a contrast with today when we can travel by train or bus and with no inconvenience.*

"There were only two shops in the village. The first school was in Park Road and is now called the Lyceum. Gradually the village grew – the Auditorium, Christ Church, Hulme Hall, and perhaps the finest building of its kind in England, the Art Gallery with its magnificent and priceless collection, a living remembrance of Lady Lever, who in her lifetime had so endeared herself to all who knew her.

"Only my colleagues who were present at the beginning of things can realise the magnificent progress which has been made. But we had many

happy times in those early days, in spite of the difficulties with which we had to contend."

Edwin Baron retired in 1938 having completed 52 years with the company.

Right: William Hesketh Lever

My Days at Birkenhead Institute 1933-1942

by Harold Beckett

I had nine very happy years at Birkenhead Institute - four in the Junior School and five in the Senior.

Miss Bowers was head of the Junior School and looked after Lower and Upper Prep. A very strong woman and a strict disciplinarian, but very fair. I learnt all about King Arthur, my times tables (essential in later life) and how to write a letter correctly by the time I was nine. Miss Booth was in charge of Form I and also ran the cubs (I was senior sixer in 1937). Form II had Miss Ashcroft (later married to Doctor Pearson) and after her Miss Gale and the glamorous Miss Pickering.

I entered Senior School in 1938 in 3A in the "Cubby Hole". This was a tiny classroom housing about 30 pupils. It was next to the gym and was originally the changing room and still had a shower in it that worked.

I remember once just before a music lesson in the gym, one unfortunate (McFarland I think) was held under the running shower for some seconds and appeared at the singing lesson dripping wet. The erudite Doctor Teasdale-Griffiths, the music teacher, ignored the whole thing!

On 3rd September 1939 I was evacuated to Oswestry along with my elder brother John and the rest of the school. He was only there four weeks and left school to enter Martins Bank. Tragically, he was killed some years later flying with the Fleet Air Arm. I think over 100 Old Boys of the Institute were killed on active service in World War II.

The stay at Oswestry was short-lived and we were back in Birkenhead by Christmas. The winter of 39/40 was very severe and the school central heating system at Whetstone Lane failed and we had lessons in overcoats, scarves and gloves. 1940 saw numerous daylight reconnaissance by German planes. I remember one summer day we were up and down to the air raid shelter, under the school in the bike sheds, 17 times!

Below: The Visor, the school badge and name of the magazine

Above: The original building in Whetstone Lane

Below: E. Wynne-Hughes, headmaster during Harold's time at the Institute.

I moved on to 4A, 5A and then 6A. Mr Paris (Johnny P) was our form master and English teacher. Maths - Bertie Bloor, Ernie Sorby and Dicky Bolton. Chemistry - Bummie Jones and Mr Davies (Porky Davvo). Woodwork - Dicky Darlington and Mr Cartwright. Geography - "Jake" Allison and Mr Thacker. History - "WEW" Williams and Biddy Harris. Physics - Mr Williams (Phizzy Whimps) and Mr Jeffries (alias Jim Brett - the Commie). Art - Mr Peter Pace. French - "Mogger" Morris. English - Jerry Hall. Gymnastics - Mr Clague and Mr Clare. The Headmaster, Mr Wynne-Hughes (The Clon) was very strict and I once got the cane - in retrospect, I deserved it!

In my last year at the school I played 1st XI cricket and 1st XV rugby and later, after I left, both soccer and rugby for the Old Instonians.

I wholeheartedly agree with Dick Bell who, writing recently in the Wirral Journal, said, *"the magic of the Institute was the relationship between masters and pupils - rapport, mutual respect, affection - call it what you will."*

I disagree entirely with Brian

> **The magic of the Institute was the relationship between masters and pupils**

Wirral Memories

"I am deeply saddened that the BI no longer exists "

Below: The school 1st XI cricket team 1942, back row, Mr Thacker, geography master, Colin Boston, A. J. Foxcroft, Bernard Jones, Joe Sudworth, Harry Brooks, Harry Gregson, Phil Harris, scorer, front, Arthur Mandy, B. E. Ware(!), Jasper Bartlett, Frank Peers and Harold Beckett.

Beard, also writing in the Journal, who said that the transition to the comprehensive system and the move to Grange was, *"generally considered to be a smooth one"*.

As for the name "Knights Grange" – which has been chosen for the housing development on the land once occupied by the Birkenhead Institute – it is absolutely meaningless. I never heard the blazer badge referred to as a "Knights Head", it was always the "Visor", hence the name of the school magazine!

Like many other Old Instonians, I'm sure, I am deeply saddened that the BI no longer exists and even more deeply saddened by the manner in which the authorities brought about the demise of the three excellent Birkenhead Grammar Schools, the Institute, Rock Ferry High and Park High.... But that's another story!

'Out of the ashes' a new 'New Brighton'

> Walking along New Brighton prom as a child, sandwiched as I invariably was between my parents, was for me both a source of nerve tingling excitement and at the same time an unwelcome initiation into that peculiar adult ceremony known as the Sunday afternoon stroll.

Below: The indoor amusement palace with its wonderfully garish and ear splitting delights.

Once out of the indoor amusement palace with its wonderfully garish and ear splitting delights, (which my parents bravely endured for my sake) there seemed little left to do but join the throng of day trippers decked out in their Sunday best, whose aimless wandering had us trailing 'sheep-like' up and down the front from 'Crazy Golf' to Bowls and back again.

Crowd dodging was never my forte and so I was jostled pushed, rammed by prams, teenagers and courting couples relentlessly entwined for the sole purpose of blocking my path. My parents, apparently oblivious of my suffering, carried on cheerfully regardless.

Yet despite (or perhaps because of) its 'Kiss-me quick' tackiness and the gradual decline in its attractions, New Brighton in the early '70s was booming. Perhaps it was the memory of its still more glorious past that drew people back long after the once bristling boarding houses had all but put up their shutters.

Perhaps it was the spectre of the once famous Tower (taller than Blackpool Tower by some 44ft), demolished in 1929, or its once splendid glass-domed ballroom raised to the ground by fire, along with the pleasure garden, in 1969.

Perhaps it was the hope that one day the fabulous roller coaster would be seen once more flying majestically and

Above: New Brighton in the early '70s was still booming, the Miss New Brighton Beauty Contest.

magically through the trees. Or perhaps it was simply that fewer people had cars then and New Brighton was one of the few places accessible by train. Whatever the reason, the crowds kept on coming.

By the time the pier had disappeared in 1978, however, the stream of visitors had dwindled to a

I was jostled pushed, rammed by prams, teenagers and courting couples relentlessly entwined for the sole purpose of blocking my path

Above: Vale Park, with its view of sloping flower banks and strips of sparkling river winking through the trees.

trickle and New Brighton fell into a state of depression, mirrored by its murky waters, polluted beach, boarded up shops and an era of growing unemployment and poverty. Its days as a thriving pleasure resort seemed numbered.

Then in the spirit of the 80's 'face lift', with the buzz word 'Development' ringing in its battered eaves, New Brighton was given a last minute reprieve. While this did not, sadly make a great impression on a depleted infrastructure, it did at least allow a new face to emerge from the ashes; one that was sparse but fresh,

pared down but spacious, and with a certain refinement to which we have become accustomed in the '90s even in our dole offices.

It has to be said that New Brighton '90s style, has become in many ways a far more interesting, if less bustling, place to park the car for the day. Apart from the black and white Victorian railings, the widened pink pavements and tonnes of imported sand, there are the mysterious silver grey stones banked along the sea wall, which despite their obvious artifice give the whole front a

bleakly Atlantic feel. On a winter's day at high tide, with the waves leaping to dramatic heights over the side, it is not difficult to picture oneself on a Britanny sea front or on the shores of the West Coast of Ireland.

There are still the few familiar relics of former times, the green and cream Art Deco buildings that house the few remaining rides, a newly installed go-kart track and, perhaps most importantly for the children amongst us, the wonder of "Adventureland", with its giant slides, fun houses, trampolines and a myriad of other bouncy soft things. Here, for a fixed fee, children can play all day (or at least for as long as their parents can stand it, which in some cases may be little more than the time it takes to read the Sunday papers!)

Once out of the din and into the light, past the whiff of salty seas and fish and chips and the host of cafes and tea shops including the excellent

intent. To begin with there are the Victorian sea front houses to pry on with their wonderful views and sloping gardens. If this holds little appeal for your ten year old, there is no need to panic and rush back in search of the nearest ice cream van!

Along the route, there are cyclists, scooter riders skate boarders, wheeled beings of all shapes and sizes to ogle at

Below: The pier had disappeared by 1978, but back in the 50s it was all bustle.

'Seaview', (featured in the last series of the Liver Birds) – is where, for me, the new New Brighton truly begins. The pedestrianised trawl towards the curling tail of Seacombe has become a freshly discovered pleasure to walk down, cycle on, jog along, or simply loiter round with little

(or better still the kids could bring their own wheels). But perhaps even more importantly, there is now a destination to aim for, a goal in sight, a carrot to jog for.

What may once have seemed an aimless, albeit pleasant ramble, reminiscent of my

own childhood Sunday strolls, has been redeemed by the discovery of the wonderfully metamorphosed Vale Park.

A pearl among parks, it has all the trendy chic of a London park, yet with a distinctly under populated Wirral feel.

Here, there is something for everyone; an imaginative playground, plenty of hills to climb, flowers to smell, a bandstand area that stages a host of feats, fairs and concerts, including the National Blues Festival and the International Guitar Festival.

But more than all this even, it has Vale Park Cafe, with its Mediterranean green floor, umbrella tables and chairs and fine freshly cooked food. Sipping coffee in the shade of one of its umbrellas on a summer's day has all the holiday charm of a sunny Spanish courtyard. With its view of sloping flower banks and strips of sparkling river winking through the trees, it is a place to bask, to listen to music, a place to relax, and if the fancy takes you a place to dream of other times, other places.

We may never see the restoration of New Brighton to all its former splendour, yet the bill boards offering 'Prime Site for Development' must hold out some hope for the birth of future delights. I see a hotel glistening with fairy lights, a 'wacky warehouse' at back, fountains out front. I see a theme park, a mini Camelot, an Alton Towers, a brave New Bright Disney Town. I see crowds, queues, car parks, day trippers by the coach load. Yes it would be wonderful (wouldn't it ?) Then again, how about a simple roller coaster that can fly through trees?

Now there's a thought...

Karen T Ward

Right: New Brighton Pool, "Britain's Wonder Pool", at the height of its popularity in the 40s.

Below: On a winter's day at high tide, with waves leaping to dramatic heights, it is not difficult to picture oneself on a Britanny sea front.

BRITAIN'S WONDER POOL

The Top Shop

The Top Shop was at the top of Village Road in Higher Bebington, where it joined Mount Road. It had windows onto both roads

FOR years The Top Shop was THE place for teenagers to meet on Sunday nights.

The Top Shop was, appropriately enough, at the top of Village Road in Higher Bebington, where it joined with Storeton (actually Mount) Road. In fact the shop had a window onto both roads. On Sunday nights, a crowd of fifteen or twenty young people would start gathering outside the little

sweet shop from about 6.30 onwards, to be joined an hour or so later by those who had been to the evening services at Christ Church on Kings Road.

Those who had been to church, especially the girls, seemed eager to catch up on what was going on - the gossip - who was going out with whom, what records we should listen to, the latest clothes the girls had bought, where the next party was to

The group would drift off across the road and down Rest Hill

> ... a wonderful place to meet girls and the girls went to be seen by the boys!

be held - all the essential information necessary to be a 'cool' teenager.

By the way, attending church was not the chore it might have been to adolescents. The boys found it a wonderful place to meet girls and the girls went to be seen by the boys.

Remember the Lonnie Donegan song "Sweet Sixteen, goes to church, just to see the boys"?

Well, he got those lines from Geoff Gardner and Dennis Smith, the pop Poet Laureates

of the Higher Beb' crowd. Come to think of it, even 'Boney Alec' Jones and Ray 'Cabby' Beech sometimes bent a knee in the back pews, while grinning sideways across the aisle at a row of comely teenage wenches.

It was well known that their personal relationship with their Lord had been somewhat less-than-personal for many years.

Within a short while, everyone had stocked up on the necessities; spearmint chews, peardrops, Mars Bars

and gum, and one or two had bought their packets of Players or Woodbines.

After milling around, accompanied by a little horseplay and chasing, the group would drift off across the road and down Rest Hill.

Sometimes the walk would only be as far as the entrance to the woods, but, if the night were clear and without the immediate prospect of a downpour, the route would be established as 'the full block'.

We would wend our massed

" The first mile and a half was dark and only one or two cars would pass us during that distance ... "

Mile Road', known to cartographers and local planners as 'Lever Causeway'

way down the hill, around past Storeton Farm and up the long, straight 'Mile Road', known to cartographers and local planners as 'Lever Causeway'. Turning up Marsh Lane and passing the farm kept by The Misses Bather, we would walk along the top road, eventually ending up back at the then closed Top Shop.

The first mile and a half was dark and only one or two cars would pass us during that distance, It was then, unnoticed by anything except owls, badgers and other nocturnal creatures, that some individuals in the group would slip/sidle/ insinuate themselves next to preselected others in the group, and begin quiet conversations.

Sweets, and occasionally cigarettes, were shared and arms would encircle shoulders or waists once or twice couples would stop and kiss. It was not considered polite to notice. We just kept on walking and talking, ambling and rambling, recounting the film we had seen the previous night at The Regal or The Rialto, or describing some terrible or supposedly exciting event that had taken place in our lives.

Despite the connived air of casual interaction, there was always an over-riding awareness of pulsing testosterone and coursing oestrogen dictating the brash, macho assertions of the gangly, spotty boys and the coy, almost coquettish, responses from the giggling, shuffling girls.

Sexuality hung heavy in the air and innuendo flew back and forth, seeking a flirty response that seemed to mean what the recipient hoped it might mean. Fantasies were either fulfilled, or dashed and put on the mental imaging back-burner for another week.

I don't know of any 'virtues' that were actually 'lost' on those Sunday night walks, and probably wouldn't comment even if I did ("let him who is without sin amongst them, cast the first...."), but I for one wouldn't have missed the expectation and anticipation that went along with going on those walks for the world.

Even though we talked casually, and outwardly seemed only interested in mixing and interacting with the group as a whole, we never took our eyes off the one, or ones, we hoped to

Above: Sometimes the walk would only be as far as the entrance to the woods.

❝ ...arms would encircle shoulders or waists and once or twice couples would stop and kiss ...❞

Above: Recounting the film we had seen the previous night at The Rialto.

link up with before the walk was over,

If Marie moved a little too close to Alan, my heart started to beat faster, Surely she prefers me? I'd better make my move, but what if she turns me down? I think I saw Val look at me, perhaps she is getting fed up with Dave?

Does Jackie kiss as well as some say she does - I'd love to find out?' These and similar questions and insecurities filled the mind of a thirteen, fourteen or fifteen year-old male, anxious to make a move yet terrified of rejection and possible humiliation in front of the pack of his perambulating peers.

No matter how often I slipped unnoticed and surreptitiously close to the one who filled my fantasies on any particular night, it seemed that someone would always say or do something that caused a re-arrangement and She would remain an elusive two or three persons away from me. I would see the end of The Mile Road coming closer. I would know that I had to make my move soon, before we re-entered the glaring yellow brightness of the overhead sodium light fixtures along Mount Road.

I can recall thinking: "I must make one more try?" Plucking up courage, I cross behind the

main group and emerge nearer to Her. Then, I find myself walking next to her; she smiles; we're talking; I catch a whiff of her perfume; she is laughing at something I said; she is looking into my eyes; our hands brush together; our shoulders are touching; now is the time - go for it!

Before I know it, we are holding hands. The contours of her belted gaberdine mac never looked so good. She squeezes my hand. I return the intimation. I slow down a little and slip my arm around her shoulder. Chanel Number Five invades my nostrils. She responds by pulling closer to me. Now my mind fills with expectation, anticipation, trepidation, daring to dream of kissing those full red lips............

During the home stretch along Mount Road, our numbers dwindled noticeably. Some had peeled off and headed for home, especially if those homes were closer to Dacre Hill or Kings Lane than they were to Village Road. Others, who had been dropping further and further behind the main gaggle of strolling teenagers as we had ambled the length of The Mile Road, had quietly peeled off in pairs, arms entwined, and dissolved into the dark anonymity of Storeton Woods. We would see them again another day.

The nice thing was, that when I got home and my Mother asked where I had been, I could honestly reply that I had been for a walk after church. (The inference was that I had actually been to church.) It was the kind of good and wholesome way of passing time that mothers approved of. Even girls' mothers felt that there was safety in numbers. I often hoped that my Mother wouldn't notice the grass stains on my knees and elbows.

The Top Shop doesn't exist anymore. It's a private house. I don't know whether the shop made any money out of the Sunday night throng and its ritual assembly there. It may well have discouraged many customers from squeezing through the pubescent mass of humanity and spending their pounds and shillings, more than offsetting the pennies, threepenny bits and the occasional sixpence, derived from that mass. The Travellers Rest across the road certainly didn't make a red cent from us, as we were all too well-known to the Landlord and he wasn't about to jeopardise his licence just to satisfy the bravado of one or two show-offs amongst us.

Anyway, we didn't have to sneak a pint at 'The Rest' - We could go any night of the week and get served at The Royal Oak - a 'men-only' pub (by custom) that had a very loose interpretation of the legal drinking age. Oh, the times we had in the old Royal Oak!   W̱M̱

But that's another story.

Gordon Ratcliff, formerly of Asterfield Avenue', now 45th Street South, St Petersburg, Florida.

The Royal Oak - a 'men-only' pub that had a very loose interpretation of the legal drinking age, little changed from this 1890s picture

Thoughts from West Kirby

I have watched in fascination as the lunar month goes by...

... Your slow but sure encroachment on the shore.
And I have wondered at what moves you to advance in such a way
Each day a little further than before.
And I have heard the sea birds squealing as you lap around their feet
Witnessed golden, ancient sands, being turned to grey
I've felt the morning mists surround you as the sun you gladly greet.
Seen you crush and crumble castles in your way.
But when the moon is past her fullness you will gradually recede
And leave us with our desert for a while.
And our castles will stand firm and strong, defiant in your sight
Until she waxes and you reclaim every mile.

Then, where we sat and played all day, without your crushing might
Will be boiling with your seething salty spume
For your time has come to conquer us, to retake what is yours
To set afresh your all encircling loom.
And weaving patterns in the sand you come, reclaiming every mound
Swirling harshly and with unabated might.
Leaving tapestries of wonder never seen by us before
Stealing through our playground in the night.
But tell us of the secret place you go to when you flow
What other shores embrace, what sights you see

Out there across your vastness, for I have the need to know
The foreign waters that you're bringing back to me?
Were I but deep within you I could follow, I could glean
The secret of your leaving us behind.
The flotsam that you toss today, where will you let it land?
As you drag it out encrusted, salted, brined.
And who will find it, where, and when, will they too sit and dream
Of the places they may never get to see?
I ask you mighty ocean as you pound my shore today.
Bring the answers to my questions back to me.

But while I wait, I'll watch in wonder as the pattern you repeat
And dream of those exotic shores, and foreign wading feet
And I will follow every moonrise and her path so clean and bright
Perhaps your secret lies within her silvery, liquid light.
One day I'll climb upon that moonbeam and I'll follow where you roam
Safe assured that as you ebb and flow, one day you'll take me home.
And I will join you on your travels, I will share the sights you see
For your wanderlust is calling and your power possesses me.

Jo Wood

Burton Village

Burton Village, today, is known to visitors and residents alike as a delightful 'olde worlde' rural village of almost picture book appearance. But Burton has been many different villages over the years.

This delightful cottage, "Bishop Wilson's Cottage", was the birthplace of Thomas Wilson, Bishop of Sodor and Man, in 1663

Now very much a desirable residential retreat, Burton, like many of the towns and villages along the Dee coast of Wirral, was once a port and a busy market town.

In the fourteenth century travellers from Wales to Lancashire would disembark here and refresh themselves in one of the hostelries before setting out across Wirral for Monks' Ferry at Birkenhead Priory then to cross the Mersey into Lancashire.

Burton's history, however, stretches back to the Domesday Book in which it was listed as "Burh Tun", or *'village near a fortified place'*. This may well have referred to the earthwork, a single rampart and ditch, at Burton Point one mile south of the village. This may have been an Iron Age hill fort or even a Celtic fortification protecting the anchorage on the banks of the Dee.

Although not obvious today, because of the silting of the Dee and the extensive reclamation work around the steel works and the shooting range, Burton Point was once a very prominent outcrop into

Top: St Nicholas' Church, dedicated to the patron saint of mariers.

Below: Rake House, on the left was "The Royal Oak" which closed after the death of Ann Medlicott in 1860.

the river affording a sheltered harbour to its south east. In 1875 many skeletons were unearthed near this place, but it is not known whether they were the victims of a battle or, possibly, the crew of a ship which had foundered in the river.

The connection with the sea is also perpetuated in the parish church, dedicated, like that of Liverpool's parish church at the Pier Head, to St. Nicholas, the patron saint of mariners.

The church originally built in Norman times was largely rebuilt in 1721 although parts of the north east corner date from the fourteenth century.

In 1831 there were 48 dwellings in the village housing 313 residents, an average of over 6 per property, clearly a considerably greater number than today! There were also, significantly, several licensed premises, a 'hangover' from the earlier days as a port and market town.

Rake House, in the village, was, for a number of years, "The Royal Oak". In 1851 it was managed by Ann Medlicott and her family and after her death in 1860 it closed. Her family had come to Burton in 1810 and ran an inn called "The Earth Stopper" before moving to "The Royal Oak". Barn End, one of the oldest cottages

possibly dating from 1450, sitting on its rock outcrop was also an inn, "The Fisherman's Arms", although it was also known as "The Noah's Ark" and, more intriguingly, "The Robbers' Den".

As recently as 1850 the village was described in Bagshaw's Directory as " ... *a township and small irregular, built village, situated in a valley, near the banks of the Dee ..... The township ... contains upwards of 1,600 acres of land, the whole of which is the property of Richard Congreve Esq, except about 25 acres, held by the trustees of the school.*"

The school referred to had been endowed in 1724 by Thomas Wilson, Bishop of Sodor and Man, who had returned to Burton, the village of his birth. It was to provide free education for the children of the parish and was completed in 1735. Thomas

Thomas Wilson's birthplace in the early years of this century.

Wilson, the son of Nathaniel Wilson, was born in 1663 in a cottage in the village which is still, externally at least, little altered to this day. The school remained active until the early years of this century when it was converted into a private dwelling.

The Manor had belonged to the Bishop of Coventry and Lichfield, and in 1753, the Rev Richard Congreve took a lease on the whole estate. In 1805 his son, also Richard, bought the manor and its estate for £9,500. He built a new Burton Hall on the site clearing away many of the very old an ancient buildings. (There were no overzealous planning regulations in those days restricting development and listing everything old as 'of historic interest' and thus many of the fine buildings which are so described today were actually built!)

In fact the present Manor,

In 1831 there were 48 dwellings in the village housing 313 residents, an average of over six per property, clearly a considerably greater number than today!

now an educational establishment, is largely the work of Henry Neville Gladstone, son of William Gladstone, who had been the prime minister in Victoria's day.

Henry bought the estate in 1903 and set about extensive remodelling and extending of the hall to produce the present day Manor. The estate, though, remained intact until just after the First

World War, when social change and financial difficulties led to the breaking up of the 1,600 acres and the sale to many developers and private individuals.

This caused much local resentment at the time, but Burton, unlike so many other villages of Wirral, was fortunate in largely retaining its character and charm through this social upheaval.

W
M

Thornton Hough

Thornton Hough was mentioned in the Domesday Book as 'Torintone', but it took its present name from the marriage of the daughter of Roger de Thornton, a landowner in the reign of Edward II, to Richard de Hoghe.

All Saints Church seen across the village green, scene of cricket matches in the summer months

THIS pretty village nestling in the centre of Wirral close to Heswall, Willaston and Raby, wasn't always the 'picture postcard' scene it is today. What we see now is the handiwork, well not literally, of two rich and powerful landowners who changed it into their dream of a rural village idyll.

The first was a Yorkshire textile manufacturer from Huddersfield, Joseph Hirst, who came to settle in Wirral in the 1860s. Some years before his arrival, Thornton Hough had been described by William Mortimer, in 1847, as ".. presenting a very unpleasant appearance, and though it possesses a few tolerably good houses, the greater proportion are of a very inferior description..."

Hirst set about building new houses and, amongst other buildings, funded All Saints Church, the Vicarage, the School and Wilshaw Terrace in Church Road. After the

Thicket Ford today largely unchanged except for the ivy. (from the 1906 view overleaf)

completion of All Saints he was disappointed to find that he could not see any of the four clock faces on the spire from his own house, so he had a fifth face added slightly higher up. Hirst's influence on the village, whilst being the first effort at modern 'garden city planning' ended shortly after with his death in 1874.

However, Thornton Hough did not rest at peace for long as, in 1891, William Hesketh Lever stepped in and purchased the Hirst Estate and most of the village with it. He subsequently rebuilt pretty well all of the village, with the exception of Hirst's new buildings and transformed it into the garden village we know today.

Its similarity to parts of Port Sunlight is not surprising since he used many of the same architects and designers who were building his larger commercial 'garden village' at Bromborough on the other side of the peninsula. He rented Thornton Manor for a short while, then purchased it and virtually rebuilt it from scratch. It remains the Lever's family home to this day.

... it remains the Lever's family home to this day

Above: This idyllic scene was photographed in 1906 in St. George's Way. The delivery horse and cart are standing outside the entrance to Thicket Ford on the left — built in 1892. In the centre background is Hirst's Wilshaw Terrace and to the right the original 'Seven Stars Hotel'. Note the 'penny farthing' pram being wheeled by the lady in the foreground, and the trousers of the workman, centre, tied just below his knees to prevent vermin running up his legs in search of tasty morsels!

The rebuilding of the village involved the demolition of many of the old and insanitary dwellings, which although quaint and picturesque, were probably unfit for human habitation. He built a new smithy, shops, the Liberal Club, later to become the Village Club, and, not to be outdone, another church - St George's.

Quite why a village the size of Thornton Hough needed two churches only Lever could tell us. He also built another school. Looking back on this period of intense development one can't help but feel there was a sense of

Best Kept Village

Below right: Looking down Neston Road towards the smithy, these homes are very reminiscent of Port Sunlight with the same decorative brick detailing, sculptured stonework, ornamental plasterwork and ornate canopies and entrances. In 1931 the Thornton Hough Women's Institute was built in the space between the end houses at left in the picture. The magnificent 'horseless carriage' with its chauffeur, (could this have been Lever's?), dates this picture to around 1905.

This is the same stretch of Neston Road c. 1890, before Lever has this row of thatched cottages replaced with the new homes in the previous picture, in 1893. The old smithy is the single storey building just beyond the road sign.

needing to 'outdo' the previous landowner in the provision of public buildings!

Lever also built Hesketh Grange for his father and his brother, J. D. Lever, bought Hirst's original home, Thornton House and, of course, rebuilt it. So the whole family were now settled in Thornton Hough.

After these two periods of frenetic building activity, virtually the only building left standing of the original village was the 'Seven Stars' public house which dated back to 1850. Every other building had been demolished, or significantly altered, by Messrs Hirst and Lever in their creation of a garden village.

It is the effect of this complete rebuilding which sets Thornton Hough apart from most of the other villages in Wirral, which by and large retain many of their very old properties mixed side by side with newer developments. In many ways, although it has won "Best Kept Village Awards" over the years, it is very artificial in that it is largely, if not completely, the creation of these two Victorian landowners. 〰

Not so much a village - more a 'New Town' of the late 19th century!

Egyptian Waterways in Wartime

In 1940, with the mounting war in North Africa requiring more and more supplies, the army sent out teams of engineers to organise and maintain the vehicles and the transport network necessary to keep the supplies moving. Among these was Len Harrow of Prenton who was to spend the next four years developing and opening routes across North Africa...

Right: Len and comrades on Christmas Day 1940 outside their tent at Tel-el-Kebir.

Left: A cargo of tentage and stationery picked up at El Shallal and having survived the cross-Africa ordeal is waiting to be off-loaded at the Misr Fluviale berth in Cairo. Map shows water and overland route from South Atlantic to North Africa.

> ## Egypt had 2,200 miles of navigable waterways, including the Nile itself ...

The Movements and Transport/Inland Waterways Transport – Royal Engineers - (IWT), section emerged in June 1940 when it became clear that conventional supply lines depending upon road transport were extremely unreliable in North Africa.

Egypt had 2,200 miles of navigable waterways, including the Nile itself, its huge Delta and many miles of canals, and so this was an obvious way of moving the vast quantities of supplies involved in a global war. From its small beginnings in early 1940, just two men, this section grew, by late 1943, into an organisation employing over 2,000 people of all ranks and many nationalities, British, Dutch, Cypriots, Indians, Seychelles Islanders and, of course, many Egyptians.

Local civilian sailing and transport companies co-operated, allowing all their vessels, tugs, feluccas, dumb barges, and dhows to be requisitioned and organised by the IWT. The Royal Engineers themselves developed special power and

A cargo of African hardwood is unloaded at the Misr Fluviale berth in Cairo.

dumb barges including some experimental types made out of concrete. A typical barge would have a capacity of 200 tons and would be towed in groups of two to six, by tugs ranging in power from 200 to 600 hp. The army also made self propelled barges with diesel or even steam engines of 100-200 hp. The feluccas and dhows moved under their own sail or were towed by the tugs.

The extent of the transport network was vast, from the very busy Nile Delta section in the north including the canals linking Cairo, Alexandria, Ismailia and Port Said, down the Nile itself as it made its way from Wadi Halfa on the Sudan border.

South of Khartoum, in the Sudan, the Nile wound down from Juba, the highest navigable port for barges. From there a combined road and river route crossed over the hills and down into the Congo and so on down another vast river network which led out into the Atlantic through Equatorial Africa.

With increased enemy activity in the Indian Ocean causing losses to shipping travelling up the east coast of Africa, the alternative of off-loading supplies from Britain and America at the mouth of the Congo and transporting

Len with Mohammed, the office manager at Misr Fluviale.

The extent of the transport network was vast, from the very busy Nile Delta section in the north including the canals linking Cairo, Alexandria ...

" ... their contribution to the eventual victory in North Africa was absolutely vital "

The quay and office staff at Misr Fluviale, Len is far right.

goods by barge up this mighty river was attractive.

Although a great deal of work was required in the handling and transfer from ship to barge to truck and back to barge, the resultant safety and the shorter ocean shipping travel made this a very practical option even though the total distance from the mouth of the Congo to Cairo was 4,423 miles!

This network was to see

cargoes of bombs, shells, bridge building equipment, vehicles, cotton-seed, sheep, cattle, wheat, sugar, nitrates, oil fuel, petrol, lubricants and even - aircraft!

To keep the North African squadrons flying, replacement aircraft were shipped out in crates from Britain and North America to the Congo.

A short distance upriver they were then unloaded and assembled at small airfields

which had been specially constructed deep in the jungle. From here the assembled aircraft were then flown overland across Africa to Cairo.

The small contingent of British Officers, NCOs and men, like Len Harrow, scattered in little ports and wharfs up and down the Nile may have felt that they were, at times, a long way from the war.

But their contribution to the eventual victory in North Africa was absolutely vital – supplies meant victory, particularly in the hostile environment of the African desert.

With thanks to Len Harrow for the information, background and photographs.

W
M

Hurricanes are removed from their crates and assembled by local workers for the flight across Africa.

Len, of 148 Durley Drive, Prenton, L43 3BB, would like to hear from anyone else who served with GVRD RASC or the 946 IWT in Egypt

Len Harrow

LEONARD Dorrien Harrow was born on 8th October 1914 at 17 Lloyd Avenue in Birkenhead. His father was Richard Gibson Harrow and his mother Elizabeth, maiden name Thomson. His unusual middle name was after General Smith Dorrien.

Len's father, Richard, had spent much of his early childhood in the Royal Liverpool Seamen's Orphanage as a result of the loss of his father, James, a shipwright on the steamship "Tagus" which had disappeared en-route from Oporto to Liverpool in April 1877.

With Len Harrow's family's nautical background, it was no surprise that, on leaving Cavendish and Bidston Avenue Schools, he should go into the offices of the Clan Line, in 1929, joining his brother Fred.

Throughout the thirties Len worked in various shipping companies in those halcyon days when the Mersey was busy, always full of ships, sailors, cargoes and smoke! They were hard times too though, the depression affecting many families on Merseyside.

But worse was to come when, in September 1939, war was declared on Germany. It was not until 6th June 1940, however, that Len was called up, his papers instructing him to report to RASC Brighton the following week.

So, like many other young men caught up in the uncertainty of war, Len became engaged immediately to his sweetheart, Jean Brobyn, who was just 21. By this time Len was a 'mature' 25.

The following week, the 13th June, he reported to RASC Brighton for initial training and to find out what his King and Country had in store for him. After two months training there he was sent to Feltham to join the 9th Vehicle Reception Depot. Then he learned that he was being sent overseas.

After an all too brief Embarkation Leave of just a week in early September, it was back into training and preparation for what lay ahead. On 10th October 1940 he sailed from Liverpool for the Middle East on "Chitral", via Capetown.

At this time the Mediterranean was controlled by the Axis forces and thus it was far too dangerous to contemplate sailing through the Straits of Gibraltar, so all shipping, even those bound for Egypt, went round the

not to be long before Len's war took a surprising turn.

Having a nautical background from his family and his job in his civvy days, he was an obvious choice to join the Movements and Transport/ Inland Waterways Transport Section - Royal Engineers - (IWT).

Len was to serve for over four years in this section, opening

on 1st February 1945 he arrived back in Greenock.

Two days later he was at the North West Ports HQ at "Overleasowe" in Eleanor Road, Bidston, and a week later, on 10th February 1945 he and Jean were married after more than four years separation.

For the next two years they lived with Jean's mother in Holm Lane but during this time put down a deposit on a new house in Durley Drive, Prenton. On 24th October 1945, their son Ken was born at Liverpool Maternity Hospital.

Len served with the NW Ports Embarkation Staff until he was eventually demobbed on 10th February 1946 at Ashton under Lyne. He then rejoined the Clan Line returning to his shipping roots.

At this time the Mediterranean was controlled by the Axis forces and thus it was far too dangerous to contemplate sailing through the Straits of Gibraltar

Cape of Good Hope up the East Coast of Africa and into the Red Sea.

Two months later, on 8th December 1940, Len and his comrades arrived in Suez at the start of their real war. For the next two months Len was with the 9th Vehicle Reception Depot which had been established at Tel-El-Kebir RASC. However, it was

and operating supply routes on the Nile and the Delta canals. During this time Len learned, by cable, of the death of his mother, Elizabeth, in July 1942.

With the war in Africa effectively over by 1945, Len was able to get a home posting on compassionate grounds, his father having sustained a broken pelvis, and

In May 1947 Len, Jean and young Ken moved into "Fair Haven" in Durley Drive, they had not been allocated a number then. Two years later their daughter Christine was born at "Fair Haven".

For the next thirty years Len worked in shipping both in Merseyside and abroad until his retirement in 1980.

In 1969, Ken married Pat Fowler and Christine married Dave Bennett.

Together, Len and Jean still live happily in 'Fair Haven', Prenton, and readily enjoy the company of their six grandchildren, Rebecca, Sarah, Nathan, Daniel, Rachel and Andrew. W M

Gould's – a family firm

The firm of Gould's started in 1904 in West Kirby as printers and stationers by Mr A E Gould and his wife Mrs F Gould.

They began printing the 'Hoylake & West Kirby News' in 1907 at 10 Acacia Grove. Mr Gould had been involved in printing and stationery some years prior to that in Warwickshire.

In 1907 the business transferred to larger premises at 15 Acacia Grove which still houses the printing works and their offices today.

After the death of Mr A E Gould in 1921 the business was carried on by his widow and three years later, in 1924, their son A J Gould joined the family business.

In 1937 a second branch was opened in Heswall in the recently completed Castle Buildings. In 1945 A J Gould took over the family firm after the retirement of his mother who continued to take a close interest in the business up to her death in 1954.

Sadly, her son A J Gould also died in the same year and so the business passed to the third generation of Goulds, to G A Gould, Gordon, who still runs the business today, although ably assisted by the fourth generation Gould, daughter Anne, who joined the family firm in 1986.

In 1993 a third branch was opened in Banks Road, West Kirby, so maintaining the family connection with the town where their first business was established almost ninety years earlier.

above, one of Gould's earliest publications from their printing works at Acacia Grove

left, no 10 Acacia Grove just after opening in 1904

Recollections of Birkenhead Market

by Wilf Wilson

The stalls outside in the old Market Square were used as a Fruit and Vegetable market.

LOOKING back in my old local history notes, I found there has been a market in Birkenhead since 1835. The first market building stood on the site of the present Westminster House complex, and also accommodated the first Town Hall, Courthouse and Prison.

In 1845 a new building was erected and opened. It was large and spacious inside and the roof was supported on tall cast iron pillars, the stalls being placed back to back in line with these. Suspended from the roof cross members, down the middle of each aisle, were large ornamental gas lamps which not only gave light but also heat which was deflected down from a canopy above the burner.

Extra stalls were placed outside, situated on the old Market Square and used mainly as a vegetable market. When permission had been granted for additional use in 1909, stalls were built and roofed in to provide accommodation for retail and wholesale horticultural produce traders.

However, some years later, due to the opening of the Mersey Tunnel in 1934 and the development of the wholesale fruit and vegetable market in Liverpool, support for this type of trading in Birkenhead ceased entirely. The use of the stalls then changed and they were used

Market Square on a Saturday Night had a 'carnival atmosphere', here seen around 1904.

as a general market and retail country produce market.

The main entrance to the market was via a flight of stone steps, and immediately above the double doors was a large two faced clock. This could be seen from both the interior and exterior of the market.

Some notable stallholders included, 'Hair Skin & Toole', who specialised in restoring hair growth as a cure for baldness. One of the cooked meat specialists was 'John J. Russell'. We always went to his stall for ham cut from the bone, and for corned beef. He also had good tripe, and my father was addicted to his Bury black puddings. Mr Russell would cut three large slices of frying ham, always a regular order, which cost 3/6d in those days. 'Waterworths' were the main fruit and vegetable dealers, although 'Wyburns' were very competitive on prices and

quality. They also had a shop in Old Chester Road, Rock Ferry. 'Houghs' of Hoylake kept an excellent assortment of confectionery, cakes and loose biscuits sold by the pound, and also very good pasties and meat pies.

There were plenty of haberdashery stalls with pots and pans hanging everywhere, crockery all displayed in large wicker baskets. One or two herbalists occupied the centre stalls selling Zam Buck, which, by all accounts, cleared up all ailments known in those days.

The outside market stalls were surrounded by large Victorian houses converted into shops of every kind. 'J.W.Haylocks' was on a corner of Market Street and Argyle Street. On the other corner stood the Market Inn. Then there was a fairly large store under the name of 'Amies', and a little further up the road was 'Murphys the Pawnbrokers',

displaying the three brass balls over the door. 'William Pyke', watchmakers and jewellers also had a shop there.

Originally two fountains stood inside, in the main aisles. Later, however, these were removed to Arrowe Park, where one of them still remains. Though badly damaged by fire in 1974, the Market Hall remained in use until the present market was opened in Grange Shopping Precinct in 1977.

During the early thirties a typical Saturday afternoon and evening would be spent as follows;-

Leave home in Higher Bebington at about 1.30pm and walk to Prenton Park to catch a tram down into Grange Road. Look around the shops and possibly visit the Hippodrome, for the Saturday afternoon matinee at 3.00pm.

Right: The market was large and spacious inside and the roof was supported on tall cast iron pillars. Suspended down the middle of each aisle, were large ornamental gas lamps.

The Hippodrome had been built in 1888 and stood in Grange Road on the site of what is now the Co-op's 'Living' department store. The first proprietor was Mr Joseph Ohmy, once a famous balloonist who performed a spectacular rope trick which involved him falling from a great height.

He also ran a circus on a site near to the old Post Office in Conway Street, and employed a famous clown named Tony Felix who once raced on stilts against an old cart-horse from the Post Office to the entrance to Birkenhead Park.

The next port of call would be the old market for a cup of tea and some 'bacon butties' before doing the weekly shop. One of the main features of the market on a Saturday night was the carnival atmosphere, with many attractions including, "beat the goalkeeper" and numerous side-shows.

Resourceful ice-cream vendors would sell hot chestnuts in wintertime. It was particularly interesting when, after 6pm, due to the lack of refrigeration in those days, the traders had to sell off cheaply all their perishable goods.

To round off the day, if funds allowed, we would visit the Argyle Theatre, then one of the country's leading music halls.

First purchased in 1867, it had long narrow galleries running down each side and a seating capacity of 800.

The Argyle was to come to a sad end on 20th September 1940 when it was badly damaged by enemy bombing.

It never reopened. After the show – which finished about 9.30pm – we would catch a tram back to Prenton Park and walk home, getting in at about 11pm, tired, but having enjoyed an exciting day out! W M

Left: The Hippodrome, built in 1888, stood in Grange Road. It was known originally as 'Ohmy's Circus' but in 1890 became The Gaiety Music Hall, later, in 1898, The Metropole and finally the Hippodrome in 1908, until closure in 1934. The Co-op's 'Living' department store now occupies the site.

Roberts Motor Pioneers

by Ursula Wilde (Roberts)

R A Roberts (Alfred)

My great-grandfather, Thomas Roberts, a farmer and horse trainer, came to Bromborough in 1889, from Denbigh in North Wales. He moved into 89 Chester Road, Bromborough, where he had four children all of whom were scholars. Later he moved to the Mews in Bromborough Village which was in fact an old stable at the back of Muffs the butcher, converted into little cottages.

This area was part of Kettlewell's farm. (Much of Bromborough was small farms on Sir William Forwood's estate. His home, Bromborough Hall, stood close to the site of the Royal Oak Hotel, the main gate being where Matalan now stands.)

Thomas' son Alfred, my grandfather, went to sea at the age of fifteen and was the only young boy to survive an attack of yellow fever which swept the ship whilst docked in America.

He was very interested in anything mechanical and the birth of the motor car was particularly fascinating to him. When he was twenty he met Emma, who was to become his wife. She, like Alfred's father, was from North Wales, and was working at Bromborough Hall as Sir William Forwood's cook.

Alfred and Emma married at St. Barnabus' in Bromborough and bought a little cottage in Bromborough Rake. They had two sons and a daughter, Ursula, my mother.

In 1925 Alfred opened his first garage at Bromborough Cross next door to where Barclays Bank stands today. The garage was a converted barn which he named Central Garage. Behind the garage was Sheridan's Blacksmiths, I can remember going as a child and watching old Mr Sheridan at the anvil, sparks flashing lighting up the darkness as he shod the horses.

The garage had one petrol pump and it was served in cans and delivered to the local gentry. Grandad also sold and repaired cycles and my mother used to do the braiding on the rear wheel so that ladies did not catch their long skirts in the spokes.

A short time later my grandfather met a local gentleman of some means, Mr Woodvine, who was impressed by my grandfather's business acumen and enthusiasm. He gave him a loan to find a site to build a purpose made garage to expand. He would then pay him back when he was 'on his feet'. The whole family were, to use my mother's words, 'over the moon' at the news as they were all very ambitious.

After a few months Alfred found the perfect site on what

Above: Alfred found the perfect site for his new garage on what is now the New Chester Road on the corner of Allport Road.

is now the New Chester Road on the corner of Allport Road. At the time though, the A41 was just a country lane meandering through farmland. Local people thought he was mad, but Alfred went ahead and they built the garage with a lovely house alongside it. my mother and her two brothers, Claude and Ken, all helped to dig the big holes for the petrol tanks. Mother recalled them as very hard years, often standing serving petrol crying with the freezing cold. Later, at the age of just fifteen, my mother would drive a car called a Minerva, taking the river pilots down Green Lane to take the boats up the Ship Canal. Amazingly, she also used to drive the local police around before they had any means of transport. My mother, also Ursula, then

went to college and qualified in accountancy, going on to run the office for many years.

During the war years, Roberts Garage kept going all through the bombing. It was very dangerous living in the house so near to the garage and the petrol tanks and my mother was under tremendous

pressure. Uncle Claude kept all the local farm machinery well maintained, and also the many army vehicles which were kept opposite the garage hidden under the trees of Carlett Park. I can also remember the Nissen Huts where the soldiers were billeted. One day a German plane was shot down close by and we rushed to inform the authorities and the pilot, who had survived, was taken into custody.

Roberts Garage continued to thrive after the war for many years until 1979 when, sadly, it went out of the family ending over 50 years in the local motor trade.

Above: Bromborough hall

Left: Bromborough village

Just An Old Man

by
George Heymans

He was just an old man, sat in the park,
His eyes dim and rheumy, his countenance dark.
With arthritic fingers wrapped over his cane,
And a corduroy cap to keep off the rain.

His stare was unblinking, his thoughts far away,
To an earlier life and a happier day.
Chuckling children, Christmas day morn,
Bright shiny paper, discarded and torn.

Pushing a swing, a piggy back ride,
The school presentation. Choking with pride.
Stories at bedtime. Cuddles so tight,
Big kiss for Daddy. God bless. Night, night.

And where are they now, those kids so adored?
Grown up and gone, down south and abroad.
With careers and worries, and kids of their own;
No time to visit. Too busy to phone.

He shuffled his feet, shifted his gaze,
Sighed deep inside as his thought patterns changed.
To lovely Mary, his darling, his wife;
The girl that he'd courted, and married for life.

So tiny and shiny and pretty and bright,
He'd eyes for no other from that very first night.
How they'd laugh together whenever they thought,
Of the disastrous nights in that first tent they'd bought.

Or the springs in the bed of their small rented flat;
And his pathetic attempts to rescue a cat.
Yes, he'd love her forever. A tear touched his eye.
Was it really four years since he'd kissed her goodbye?

A knobbled old hand reached into his coat,
To feel for a tissue, as he cleared his throat.
"I'm too sentimental for my own good today,
But what else is left as the time slips away?"

Wallasey Village

a refuge for those seeking to escape the invading Saxons

This picture was taken in 1903 at the junction of Perrin Road, on the right, looking along The Village towards Leasowe Road. The first block of shops on the right includes Salisbury's the greengrocers, whose handcart is strategically placed in the centre of the road to gain maximum publicity. Clearly traffic wasn't a problem in 1903! The white building just beyond, sticking out into the road is the Black Horse Hotel. This building dated back to 1722 and was reputedly named after a famous horse which successfully ran at the nearby Leasowe Racecourse. It was demolished in 1931 when the road was widened and the present building was rebuilt back from the road. The shops opposite are on the corner of Stonehouse Road and today they are nos, 75-79. The Parish Church Hall was built on the land behind the wall on the left a few years later in 1906.

WALLASEY was mentioned in the Domesday Book as 'Walea' or 'Island of Welshmen'. So called because the area was almost totally cut off from the rest of the Wirral by what later became known as Wallasey Pool.

This small 'island' with its rocky outcrops and easy look-out points became a refuge for those seeking to escape the invading Saxons.

In later years its ready access to the river and the sea, its many suitable landing points and its relative inaccessibility made it a haunt of smugglers. It was not until the early nineteenth century that

Here again we see The Village, but a few years later in 1909 and looking in the opposite direction back towards the Black Horse from the junction of St. John's Road on the left. The block of shops on the left include the North and South Wales Bank, now the Midland. The lamppost with the drinking trough around it stood at the Leasowe Road junction and beyond, screened by trees, was Lawton's Farm with its thatched roof and tall chimneys. This was demolished the following year to be replaced with the block of shops which stand on the corner to this day. the milk cart in the foreground stands outside an antique shop and next door the paraphernalia hanging outside the shop indicates it to be an ironmonger. Note the early, and very tall, telegraph pole!

Wallasey became popular as a residential area.

With the development of the docks in Wallasey Pool forming East and West Float, and the construction of the associated rail and road links, access to the 'island' of Wallasey became much easier.

Previously the Pool and the marshes from Bidston to Leasowe had made access to Wallasey very hazardous, thus adding to its sense of isolation.

Its fine views over the river and its miles of golden sands, however, made it attractive to merchants and successful traders from Liverpool, from where they could keep an eye on movements of shipping in the river and at the same time enjoy the fresh air and pleasant beaches of the area.

This was in marked contrast to the industrial grime of Liverpool just across the river. New Brighton, itself, gradually developed into a resort with fine villas and the beginnings of seaside entertainments.

On the Wirral side of the hill looking across the marshes of Bidston, Leasowe and Moreton was the village of Wallasey itself.

... fine views over the river and miles of golden sands made it attractive to merchants and successful traders from Liverpool

"Wallasey gradually developed into a resort with fine villas and the beginnings of seaside entertainments"

By the turn of the century Wallasey Village had grown into a centre of residential and commercial activity for a large proportion of the population of the area. New shops, inns and banks were established along the length of The Village, as the main street became known, between The Breck and Grove Road.

Fine new housing, churches and parks were being built up and over the hill by builders taking advantage of the views and the easier access.

W
M

Looking down Leasowe Road from The Village, some years later, the lamppost is still there but the drinking trough in the centre has gone.

Thomas Francis and the Puzzle Stones

The tower on the right with the castellated walling around in Bebington's Village was the home of Thomas Francis. This photograph was taken in the early years of this century.

ONE of Wirral's most eccentric characters was probably Thomas Francis of Bebington. Born in 1762, he was a stone-mason and building contractor, and reputably designed and built some fine houses. Little, however, is known and the identity of these remains a mystery.

Evidently his business must have prospered, for he was able to build a substantial house for himself at The Village in Lower Bebington.

In 1885, the American Consul in Liverpool, Nathaniel Hawthorne, visited Bebington and was intrigued by this strange residence. He wrote " *In the Village we saw a house built in imitation of a castle with turrets in which an upper and under row of cannon were mounted... On the wall there were eccentric inscriptions cut into slabs of stone, but I could* *make no sense of these... We peeped through a gate and saw a piazza beneath which appeared to stand the figure of a man. He appeared advanced in years and was dressed in a blue coat and buff breaches with a straw hat on his head. Behold, too, the figure of a dog sitting chained. Also close beside the gateway another man seated. All were images and the dwelling with the inscriptions and queer statuary was probably the whim of some half crazy person*".

The cannons mounted by Thomas were of timber, reputedly for the purpose of deterring the French from invading Bebington. In this they were evidently successful for there is no record of there ever being any French occupation!

The *'eccentric inscriptions cut into slabs of stone'* refers to what were later to be known as the 'puzzle stones'. Apparently, Thomas, being a very busy man, became somewhat disturbed at young men particularly, seemingly loitering around with nothing to do outside his house. So he carved some inscriptions onto slabs of stone and built them into his garden wall so that they were visible to these 'loiterers'. No doubt it gave him great satisfaction to watch the puzzlement on their faces as they tried to make sense of these seemingly nonsensical carvings.

The first one, on the right in the photograph, puzzled them until they realised that reading across from the top it said, *"a rubbing stone for asses"*!

The second, in the middle of the picture, far from being nonsense, was a sophisticated mathematical conundrum. *"Subtract 45 From 45 That 45 May Remain"*. The solution to this seemingly insoluble sum is that 9 8 7 6 5 4 3 2 1 = 45, (when added together.) Likewise 1 2 3 4 5 6 7 8 9 = 45. Subtracting the smaller number from the larger 987654321 – 123456789 = 8 6 4 1 9 7 5 3 2. This similarly totals 45!

So, there you have it.

The third puzzle stone, on the left, depicts a building with a sign outside, clearly a pub. *"My name And sign is thirty Shillings just, and he that will tell My Name Shall have a quart on trust For Why is not Five the Fourth Part of Twenty the same in All Cases"*. This apparent jibberish is easily explained when one appreciates from the building depicted and the reference to "Shall have a quart", that it refers to a pub and its publican. The pub is

the two crowns and the publican was a Mark Noble. Two crowns were worth ten shillings, a Mark was 13s 4d and a noble was 6s 8d. These totalled – 30 shillings!

Simple isn't it? However, we do not know what the second part referring to *"...Fourth Part of Twenty..."* refers to. Any answers?

There was also another larger stone which was clearly a poignant memory of a lost love. This seems to have disappeared. However, from records it stated, *"IN S MemOR yof Kathe Ry Neg Ray cHang'd FRO mab USyli Feto li Fele SSClay"* Respacing, and appreciating that the first 'S' was in a box, or field, and thus fenced in or "acred", we find *"In sacred memory of Katherine Gray, changed from a busy life to lifeless clay"*.

Unfortunately the house and

the adjoining properties were demolished as part of the road widening scheme in the 60s.

However, thanks to a little foresight, some of the puzzle stones were saved and were built into the stone wall at the entrance to Mayer Park where they can be seen to this day.

Sadly, they are now becoming extremely weathered, and

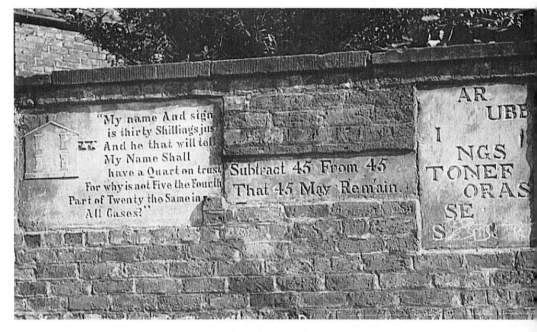

Three of the puzzle stones are seen here in their original position in the garden wall of his property.

consideration is being given to moving them to an inside location and restoring them.

Thomas Francis' eccentricity was not confined to just his carvings. He also had a reputation as a practical joker. It is reputed that he would invite guests to dine with him, at his huge dining table, to reveal with a flourish from under the lid of an enormous silver serving dish, ... a trussed sparrow! He would then proceed to carve it with great solemnity. The reaction of his guests is unrecorded but obvious.

During a period of drought he had a well dug for the benefit of the local residents. The carving pictured illustrates Thomas striking the stone and water coming forth to be collected by a small woman with a pitcher. The inscription below reads "*The people of Bebington murmured for want of water and God gave them water*". Quite whether Thomas considered himself to be 'God' is not clear, but he was definitely larger than life!

He had obtained permission from St. Andrews Church to dig his own grave in the churchyard, which he then lined with masonry. It was his custom to brush this out on a Saturday night, and then smoke his pipe in it.

Some years before his death he also had coffins made to measure for his wife and himself by a Mr Walter of Birkenhead. These he kept against the wall in his dining room and would always spend part of his birthday lying in his, and would compel his wife to do the same in hers.

From time to time the coffins had to be altered to accommodate their increasing girth, but Thomas would not pay for them until they were complete and the tops finally screwed down. Thomas finally passed away in 1850 at the age of 88, but there is no record of Mr Walter receiving his final payment.

Left: The carving illustrates Thomas striking the stone and water coming forth to be collected by a small woman with a pitcher. The inscription below reads "The people of Bebington murmured for want of water and God gave them water".

You'll still be there tomorrow

by
Lili Lace

Oh, what can I say, it's been another day,
With lots more bills to pay, will they never go away?
Not a chance — they will always be there,
But that's the kind of life we share.

For many years we've been together,
We've got ourselves through some stormy wheather.
Since tying the knot we've never looked back,
We started out in what seemed a shack.

Looking back at what we've been through,
But what we did we always knew.
I love you more than anything now,
But how we did it, only we know how.

Two beautiful daughters made from love,
We were truely blessed from heaven above.
If the question where would I do it again,
Everything we did, I would just do the same.

The letters you write, are just sheer delight,
I read them, when in my bed at night.
And when I lay my head upon my pillow,
I know that you'll be there tomorrow.

I know you will never leave me, so I'll never cry,
I will never wipe any tears from my eye.
I adore everything you do,
I know that you know it — but I still love you.

Floating Magazine Company

In June 1996, Antony Broad from Dorset gave Wirral Champion readers a real challenge — this is Antony's original letter and our reply ...

The magazine ship "Swallow" around 1925.

Dear Editor,

THE archivist on the Wirral at Birkenhead suggested I might write to you to see if any of your readers might know about, or have relations who worked for, the Liverpool Floating Magazine Company.

My great uncle, Frank Paul, was at a picnic held on 21st June 1884 at Hooton Wood. He was a surgeon in Liverpool and a member of the Mersey Canoe Club.

Looking at a sequence of photographs in an album it is clear that my great uncle and three friends were involved in the picnic.

The staff of the Liverpool Floating Magazine Co lived in a series of cottages near the

> ## Sadly, all traces of the cottages and the village have now disappeared

Mersey at Bromborough. The magazine was a ship moored for safety in the centre of the River Mersey.

On the same day as the picnic, my great uncle stopped at Bromborough to take photographs of Mr John Earl and his family. He is described as the manager of the Liverpool Floating Magazine Company.

The picnic took place in the afternoon and evening and the four photographs that survive show some twenty or so people. I know from the 1881 census that some of the men who worked for the magazine are called, Leay, Whittle, Bird, McGraw and Norbury.

My great uncle's friends were an architect called Henry Bare, and two doctors, Davies Colley and John D. Hayward the latter of whom had a practice in Liverpool.

Does anyone recognise any of these names or know of anyone who worked for the Magazine Co?

Yours sincerely,

Antony Broad, Dorset

Dear Antony,

Sorry, I am unable to help you with your enquiry. However, I can supply a little more detail of the background and I also include a photograph of one of the 'floating magazines', the "Swallow".

It was on board these vessels that the black gunpowder, manufactured by the Magazine Company which, surprisingly, was based in London, was stored for safety reasons. There were, in fact, three of these specially constructed vessels, each little more than a large barge, which were moored at various times in the Eastham Channel of the River Mersey with their highly dangerous cargoes. The other two vessels were the "Liverpool" and the "Mersey".

At its peak, the village consisted of fifteen cottages housing the workers of the company. In the thirties, the village gradually fell into disrepair as the business closed down. The land, at the bottom of what was appropriately named 'Magazine Road', which had been leased by the company for 99 years from 1853, reverted to Lever Brothers in 1952. All traces of the cottages and the village have now, sadly, disappeared, and the site is now occupied by the successful local engineering company, McTay's, as their boatyard.

The "Swallow" was the last of the 'floating magazines' to survive and, ironically, it was finally broken up on the shore in front of the village.

Yours, Editor

Mr John Earl and family by Frank Paul, 21st June 1884

The Forgotten Army
W.L.A. Timber Corps

By Muriel Bader

Bala 1942, Muriel Bader, standing left with, Peggy, Eileen and Terry. Front l to r, Elsie, Kathleen, Gwen and Ida. Where are you now girls?

I WAS 17 when war broke out and shall never forget when Liverpool was blitzed. An incendiary bomb came down our chimney in Wavertree and set the living room on fire, I was trapped and had to run through the flames losing my eyebrows, eyelashes and the front of my hair, thus suffering burns to my face, hands and legs made worse by the fact that I was covered in soot which had burnt into the skin.

When I was due to be "called up" at the age of 19, it was the munition factory for me, so I decided to volunteer for the 'Timber Corps' which I had seen on a poster somewhere. I passed my medical and was accepted.

The uniform was the same as the W.L.A. (Women's Land

> **After the first week we began to feel human again as our hands and muscles hardened up**

The lumberjacks were on piecework and each tree had to be measured lengthways and around the girth once they had trimmed off the branches ...

Army), but we had a green beret. I was issued with a pair of breeches, one green jumper, two shirts, 2 pairs of woollen socks and a pair of strong brown shoes. Later on I was to secure my overcoat, in the meantime I had to wear my own. I also received a pair of black lace-up boots and heavy gum boots, we had to supply our own underwear etc, for which we were allowed a few clothing coupons!

I set off in March 1941 to beautiful Bala in North Wales where I was 'billeted' in a pub, the first time I had set foot inside one!

We went to work up in the hills, overlooking Bala Lake, in the back of an open lorry come rain or come shine, whilst the Italian prisoners of war, who were working on the farms, had a nice covered lorry with seats! We were eight girls in number from all walks of life and most of the lumberjacks were Welsh and local.

The first day we were set to work sawing pit props and cross-cutting large timbers and de-barking trees for telegraph poles which had to be perfect in shape. We ached

in every muscle and our hands were red raw. We hardly had the strength to climb back on the lorry home.

After the first week we began to feel human again as our hands and muscles hardened up. We took sandwiches for lunch which we ate in the open around a fire where we boiled our 'Billy-cans'. There was usually a stream or a spring where we could get water. The men often used to sing after lunch and it was lovely to hear those beautiful voices. They tried to teach us some of the Welsh songs so we could join in.

We had no toilet facilities whatsoever, so we always had to sneak away in twos when nature called, one as look-out in case anyone appeared unexpectedly!

We had no shelter at all and had to work in all weathers, often up to our knees in mud. Gloves were useless but I never had a chilblain despite the bitter cold.

The lumberjacks were on piecework and each tree had

to be measured lengthways and around the girth once they had trimmed off the branches. This was a difficult job and often dangerous as the tree could move whilst we were clambering about, we were working on very steep slopes. The branches also had to be cleared and stacked then burned, a popular job in the winter!

We received the princely sum of between £2-10-0 and £2-15-0 a week, of which we paid £1-10-0 a week for our digs. I myself also had to send home 15 shillings per week leaving very little to buy washing powder, soap, fares home etc. But I would not have changed those three happy years for anything.

It was an experience never to be forgotten, especially the bugs in one bed and the dirty nappies in the bath! W M

Badge of the Timber Corps of the W.L.A.

Hilbre Island

HILBRE Island, or more correctly Hilbre Islands, for there are now three distinct separate islands, have been used by man for a multitude of purposes over the centuries. They have been lived on, worshipped on, worked on, harboured beside, rescued from, fought over and finally played on. Their history is as varied as the history of Wirral itself, and in some ways is a microcosm of their larger neighbour. Their position in the Dee estuary has had a profound effect upon the way in which they have been used, occupied, altered and changed, not only by man, but by the elements themselves.

There is evidence of Bronze Age settlement and Roman occupation, and in Saxon times it was a place of pilgrimage. In pre-Norman conquest days, it is believed that a small religious house was set up on the single island, as it then was, in the name of St Hildeburgh, a corruption of the seventh century St Edburge. Some argue that this is where the present name 'Hilbre' comes from. It is known for certain that a church existed on the island prior to 1086 as both the church and the island were given to French monks in that year by Robert de Rodelent.

The monks later sold the island to Chester Abbey but it was subsequently seized forcibly by the Earl of Chester and given to his clerk. In 1230, however, Chester monks regained control of the island and retained it as part of the parish of St Oswald, maintaining a small chapel or cell, dedicated to the Virgin Mary, for centuries until 1536.

The historian John Leland wrote in 1530 of "*a celle of monks of Chester, and a pilgrimage of our Lady of Hilbyri*". Later in 1575, a local writer recorded that the Abbot of Chester maintained two monks on the island, fishing and praying! The cell, or small building, remained, although unoccupied, well into the nineteenth century.

In medieval times the island became important militarily due to its strategic position at the entrance to the Dee, which was the centre for shipping particularly to Ireland. As early as possibly the thirteenth century a beacon had been maintained on the island by the monks for the guidance of mariners, for which the Earl of Chester paid 10s per year.

From Tudor times onward Hilbre and the adjacent Hoyle Bank were to form a naturally sheltered harbour and deep anchorage for larger shipping which could no longer navigate the Dee as far as Chester.

Indeed, in the sixteenth century, despite the ecclesiastical landlord, there was even an inn on the island for the benefit of the matelots.

As recently as the early nineteenth century, there were proposals to develop these islands and the nearby anchorage at Hoyle Lake into a port with docks, harbour and warehouses as a deep water seaport to rival the then

growing claims of fast-expanding Liverpool. The Horse Channel which approached the north Wirral Coast from the Irish Sea was still considered to be the safest approach and, of course the lighthouses of Hoylake and Leasowe also made navigation easy.

Fortunately, for residents of modern Hoylake and West Kirby, this scheme got no further than the drawing board as Liverpool rapidly expanded as the Crosby Channel became the principal deep water access to the Mersey and the Hoyle Lake gradually silted up, a fate similar to that of the Dee.

Over the last two centuries, however, Hilbre retained its connection with shipping and navigation. In 1828 the Trustees of the Liverpool Docks leased the island from the Church and erected a telegraph station and tide gauges there. The telegraph station was built on the site of the old mariners' inn and even incorporated some of its original structure. In 1856 the

island was eventually purchased outright, so ending nearly eight centuries of unbroken ecclesiastical control. The buoy station, which had been established in 1836 by Trinity House, operated until 1876 when it was replaced by a new one at Holyhead.

The telegraph station and buoy station were followed, in 1849, by the lifeboat station. This station was built, together with its slip, by the Dock Trustees at a cost of £1,200. This was to be an alternative deep-water station so that the Hoylake crew could launch a lifeboat at low tide, so avoiding the previous arduous task of dragging the cumbersome vessel across the sands from the lifeboat house on the front at Hoylake. The

crew would be summoned to the island by a pair of cannon mounted on the island, which continued in use until 1890 when they were replaced by rockets.

The Royal National Lifeboat Institution took over in 1894 until the eventual closure of the station in 1939.

After the closure of the station and the later end of the second war, the usefulness of the island nautically disappeared altogether and, in 1945, it was sold to Hoylake U.D.C. It is now a bird sanctuary and site of special scientific interest (SSS) administered by the Department of Leisure Services of Wirral Borough Council.

Above: The buoy keeper's house and store built in 1836 became a club for bachelors upon its closure in 1876. The Hilbre Island Club which admitted no ladies closed in 1931.

Right: The lifeboat house and slip in this 1920s photograph appear to have an estate agent's 'For Sale' board adjacent!

A CHEERFUL OLD SOUL.

IS IT POSSIBLE

for a woman with increasing years to do laundry work. Thousands who would have been laid aside under the old system of washing have proved what

SUNLIGHT SOAP

can do in reducing labour. The cleansing properties of SUNLIGHT SOAP save years of arduous toil. Reader, prove SUNLIGHT SOAP for yourself.

BEWARE.—Do not allow other Soaps, said to be the same as the "SUNLIGHT SOAP," to be palmed off upon you. If you do you must expect to be disappointed. See that you get what you ask for, and that the word "SUNLIGHT" is stamped upon every tablet, and printed upon every wrapper.

Not so Glorious?

In 1940 in the Norwegian Sea five ships fought a one sided battle — 58 years on the ripples still lap on a nation's conscience

HMS Glorious, built in 1917 but converted to a carrier in 1930

JUNE 8th 1940 will live long in the memories of those associated with the naval action which took place on that fateful day in the cold waters of the Norwegian Sea close to the Arctic Circle.

HMS Glorious, an ageing aircraft carrier, accompanied by two destroyers, Acasta and Ardent, was steaming back home carrying a precious cargo of 25 fighter planes

desperately needed to bolster the defence of England in the Battle of Britain.

The planes had originally been taken over to Norway to assist in the fight against the German invasion but, driven back to the northern tip of the country, they, along with the Norwegian Royal family, dignitaries, some refugees and 24,500 allied troops were evacuated and embarked on a

convoy to take them back to safety in Britain.

King Haakon and his family were placed on the fast cruiser, HMS Devonshire, which set off on a different course from the main convoy. The convoy was escorted by two aircraft carriers, the Glorious and the Ark Royal, the battleship Valiant, fourteen destroyers and a couple of cruisers. At 0300 on

Glorious in 1938

Granted, in 1940 there was a war on and secrecy was essential...

8th June, the Glorious, together with destroyers Acasta and Ardent, left and set off for home ahead of the main convoy. This was to take them, fatefully, just 13 hours later, into the clutches of the pride of the German navy, the two battle cruisers, Scharnhorst and Gneisenau.

In an all too brief encounter the British ships were outgunned and sunk by a totally superior force. As a result of the action over 1500 men died, left in Arctic waters to perish of exposure – just 41 survived out of the 900 or so who were able to take to the lifeboats, in this the worst naval disaster of the war.

official reasons

But it need not, and it should not, have happened if sense had prevailed in the upper echelons of that most senior service.

Today, the Ministry of Defence will tell you the reasons for the disaster – the official reasons, that is.

They will says that no-one is to blame, it was purely bad luck and unfortunate circumstances ...

1. Glorious, Ardent and Acasta left separately because Glorious was "short of fuel" and could not wait the extra day to sail in the safety of the large main convoy.

2. The presence of the German battle cruisers was "unknown to the Admiralty".

3. The desperate wireless messages from Glorious, sent as she was attacked, went unheard or were "garbled and unreadable" by the nearest allied ships, including the Devonshire, which was, anyway, "100 miles away".

4. The plight of the survivors, consequently, wasn't known until days later when they were subsequently picked up by Norwegian trawlers.

reality different

The reality, however, was very different.

Through the persistence of survivors, relatives and others concerned with the truth, through requests in the press for information, through examination of documents which have been released, (some are still closed for 75 years and many were originally marked "closed till 2041") a different picture emerges and it does our navy and our nation little credit;-

Granted, in 1940 there was a war on and secrecy was essential, but our then enemies are now our European allies, there is little to protect by the continuation of this official 'cover-up' other than the reputation of the senior service and some senior personnel ...

1. Glorious and her escorts did not leave the convoy because of 'SHORTAGE OF FUEL'. Indeed, the escorts themselves had refuelled only the previous day from a tanker off Harstaad, as Glorious also could have done should it have been necessary. Ark Royal, a similar sized vessel with comparable fuel capacity and consumption, was not short of fuel and the two aircraft carriers had sailed

together from Scapa Flow just nine days earlier. So why was Glorious "short of fuel"? Interestingly, no document or message from that period ever referred to "shortage of fuel".

Indeed, it didn't emerge as the official 'reason' until May 1946 when heated questions concerning the disaster were raised in the House of Commons. In a carefully worded reply to a member Mr Dugdale, Financial Secretary to the Admiralty, cited this as the reason that Glorious departed early.

Even Winston Churchill, in writing his war histories in 1948, was sceptical, *"This explanation is not convincing. The Glorious presumably had enough fuel to steam at the speed of the convoy. All should have kept together."*

real reason

No – the real reason was that the captain, Guy D'Oyly-Hughes, was anxious to return to Scapa Flow to prepare for the Courts Martial of his senior Fleet Air Arm officer, Commander J B Heath. So violently had they disagreed over flying tactics on a previous operation that as a result the captain had suspended Heath and had left him back at Scapa. Indeed, a captain of one of the other convoy destroyers, HMS Diana, had seen Glorious signal Ark Royal, on the night of June 7th, requesting permission to "proceed ahead to Scapa Flow to make preparations for impending Courts Martial". That captain, who was later to become

Commander Le Geyt, is now dead, but in 1968 he was serving in the Intelligence Division of the navy and quite by chance came across the secret, still closed report on the 1940 loss of the three ships. In view of his direct association with the incident some 28 years earlier, he was naturally very interested and noticed the reported reason for the ships' departure from the convoy. Concerned at this 'inaccuracy' in the report he added a hand written note in the margin referring to the signal which he, personally, had seen relayed to Ark Royal on the night of 7th June 1940. Despite his high rank, his obvious integrity and his concern, this 'flawed recollection' has been officially 'rubbished' by the navy ever since!

Also, fatefully, as a direct consequence of the suspension of Commander Heath, there was no senior Fleet Air Arm officer in a position to argue with the captain over flying activities.

2. The presence of the German naval forces in the Norwegian Sea WAS known

to the Admiralty. Indeed, the 'boffins' at Bletchley Park listening station had been monitoring German naval transmissions and had warned the Admiralty that it all pointed to a major task force being on the move and to warn ships in the Norwegian Sea. But these 'boffins' were just 21 year old university graduates, what did they know of naval intelligence?

Harry Hinsley was one, later to become Professor Sir Harry Hinsley the doyen of the intelligence services, who led the team which cracked the Enigma codes. Even up to his recent death, earlier this year, he was still angry at the unnecessary loss of all those lives, "On that day, more so than ever, I was saying for Goodness sakes, can't we persude them just to send an alert?"

3. Perhaps the biggest element of the 'cover-up', though, is the denial that wireless transmissions were picked up by ships near enough to help. When Glorious, belatedly, spotted the German ships she sent an emergency message which WAS picked up by

"This explanation is not convincing. The Glorious presumably had enough fuel to steam at the speed of the convoy. All should have kept together." Winston Churchill, 1948

Chart of the action from "Loss of HMS Glorious" by Vernon Howland, Capt, RCN rtd. (pub. 1994)

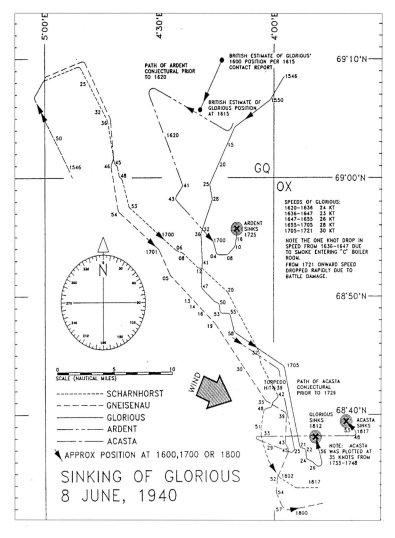

SINKING OF GLORIOUS
8 JUNE, 1940

Devonshire some way to the west on her lone mission. Two Wireless Telegraph operators on Devonshire and the Admiral's signalman, who was on the bridge at the time, confirm that they read the message which was both clear and obvious, referring to PBs (pocket battleships), giving position and speed. Indeed the Vice-Admiral and the Captain, after plotting Glorious' radioed position, were in an extremely 'agitated' state and, despite orders to maintain radio silence because of the importance of their 'cargo', signalled the Admiralty for immediate instructions. Further, the captain gave the order to "exercise main armament" indicating there was an immediate surface threat.

almost a riot

It is even alleged that King Haakon himself implored the captain to ignore his presence and take whatever action he felt was appropriate. Some time later, though, they received a reply to their signal from the Admiralty confirming that they were to carry on home at speed. By this time, though, news of Glorious had spread throughout the ship and the

decision to carry on almost led to a riot, particularly since the lookout had seen two mast-tops on the eastern horizon, just 30 miles distant – which must have been Scharnhorst and Gneisenau. Mysteriously, later in the day the W/T officer was asked by the senior officer on board, Vice-Admiral John Cunningham, for the copy of the message and the original operator's log, neither of which have been seen to this day.

4. The possibility, indeed probability, of the loss of the ships and the consequent likelihood of survivors in the icy water must have been obvious to the Admiralty because of Devonshire's request to go to their assistance. Indeed, the following morning some of the survivors reported a Walrus aircraft flying over without, apparently, spotting them. This aircraft must have come from Ark Royal since she was the only other carrier in the area and most of the Norwegian airfields were by then in German hands. (It later transpired that the Walrus crew had been instructed to search for "a pocket battleships and two destroyers" – little chance, then, of them spotting the small liferafts and floats of survivors!)

Further, the following day Lord 'Haw Haw', on German propaganda radio directed at Britain, gloated over the sinking of the Glorious and her escorts. Amazingly, later the same day the main

Why... does the MoD persist in putting forward this unrealistic explanation?

convoy, which was seen by many of the survivors, sailed through the area of the disaster without, seemingly, looking for them.

epilogue

It is clear that at the time the instruction to the Devonshire to proceed home was seen as the only sensible option. She could have done little to help Glorious and her escorts with her smaller armaments against the might of the German battle cruisers – she would probably have suffered the same fate as Glorious – blown out of the water before getting in range – and her cargo was indeed valuable.

On the other hand, with the benefit of hindsight, it has been argued that although she might not have been able to take any active part in the conflict, Devonshire would have been in an ideal position to pick up the survivors, as, in the event, immediately after the sinkings, Scharnhorst, damaged by a torpedo from Acasta, was making for Trondheim accompanied by Gneisenau. Indeed, German sources since the war have confirmed the deep

unhappiness of the German crew at having to abandon the survivors, fellow seamen, in the icy waters. However, due to the damage to Scharnhorst it was considered too risky to attempt to pick them up because of the proximity of other "allied naval vessels".

But many questions still remain unanswered ...

1. Why did an aircraft carrier with 25 planes on board, 5 of which were stated to be "at 10 minutes readiness", fail to get a single one off in the half hour before she was so severely damaged that it was then impossible?

2. Why didn't she, anyway, have at least one aircraft on permanent reconnaissance, a standard procedure at the time when in hostile waters?

3. Why, on a clear high visibility day, did she not have a lookout in the crow's nest?

4. Why did Admiral Wells of Ark Royal readily agree to D'Oyly Hughes' seemingly trivial request which thus risked three ships and so many men and, consequently, also halved the possible aircraft cover for the main convoy and its 24,500 troops?

5. Why, in view of the state of war, was there any surprise at enemy ships being in the area?

6. Why, in the light of the message received by Devonshire and the lookout's subsequent siting of the mast-tops, wasn't the ensuing 'silence' of Glorious, Ardent and Acasta seen as a probable loss?

7. Why, with most of the senior personnel now dead, and much of the documentation in the public domain, does the MoD persist in putting forward this unrealistic explanation?

One last thought......

There is a sinister alternative which has been propounded by some of those involved.

sacrificed?

Were Glorious and her escorts deliberately sacrificed to divert the German battle cruisers away from Devonshire and her valuable 'cargo' which was so perilously close, and towards which they were heading? Indeed, if the battle cruisers had not met Glorious and her two escorts they would very shortly have seen the Devonshire. After all, the lookout on Devonshire saw them!

I am indebted to the work and notes of the following ...

Sam Farrington (who lost a brother on Glorious), Tim Slessor (whose father was senior FAA officer on Glorious), Gerard Salt (who lost his elder brother on Glorious), Ben Barker (the grandson of captain of Ardent), John Winton (the author of "Carrier Glorious" pub. 1986), Trevor Jenkins (the wireless/telegraph operator aboard Devonshire) but particularly to Fred Thornton, one of two local survivors, who lent me his volume of documents on this tragic affair.

A Glorious Memorial?

DESPITE the enormity of the disaster and the extent of the tragedy, the sinking of Glorious and her two escorts is, surprisingly, not specifically commemorated by any official memorial.

There is, however, one small memorial which indirectly refers to the hundreds of souls who perished in those icy seas in 1940. A commemorative stained glass window in memory of Lt Commander Hugh Parkin is set in the wall of the small parish church of St Peter in Martindale. It was given to the church by his widow and dedicated by the Bishop of Carlisle in 1976.

The parish church of St Peter, Martindale

Commander Parkin had lived locally and this individual memorial in his own parish church in this quiet corner of Cumbria, near Patterdale, has become a focus of attention for survivors, researchers and relatives alike in the years since.

The window itself is in the form of an aircraft carrier ploughing its way through the sea depicting the ship's badge, an anchor and a phoenix rising from the flight deck.

At the base, below the bible, is the simple inscription, "In memory of Lt Commander Hugh Parkin, Fleet Air Arm RN, and the officers and men killed in action. HMS Glorious sunk in Norwegian waters, 8 June 1940".

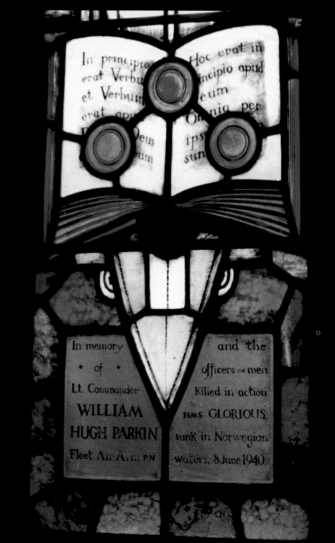

Right: The dedication at the base of the window

Ark Royal
The Wirral connection

From the deck of a Birkenhead ferry, Ark Royal is seen here in the Mersey, in late 1937, just after her fitting out was completed.

HMS Ark Royal, which figured significantly in the Glorious incident, had Wirral connections. Indeed, she was built at Cammell Lairds and was launched on 13th April 1937. Over the following 16 months she was fitted out in Laird's basin just in time to be commissioned at the start of the war in September 1939.

She was the most modern carrier of her time, with a complement of 1,575 officers and men. Displacing 22,000 tons and 800 feet long, she was the first ship actually designed as an aircraft carrier. Previously carriers, like Glorious, had been converted to that role from that of light battle cruisers when the advantage of marine air power became clear.

Ark Royal could carry up to 72 aircraft, mainly Blackburn Skuas and Fairey Swordfish, although, due to shortages of suitable aircraft in the early years of the war she never actually had more than 54 on board at any time. Whereas Glorious, Furious and Courageous, the three converted carriers, had limited capacity of 36-48 aircraft maximum.

All four, though, had similar speeds, 30 knots, and range. During the war she was involved in many famous battles including tracking the

Ark Royal... new and purpose-built

Graf Spee, the sinking of the Bismark and supporting Malta during the seige of 1941. But her war, too, like that of Glorious, was all too short.

She was torpedoed by U81 in the Mediterranean, eventually sinking just off Gibraltar, on 13th November 1941, just 27 months after commissioning. It is startling when one considers that it took over four years of sweat and toil by thousands of men to construct her, and then her 'active life' was just a little over two years, brought to an abrupt end by the small crew of a U Boat! That sinking too, though, is not without its critics. Afterwards, at the official enquiry it was suggested by some in authority that her Captain and crew were too eager to leave her and with a little forethought and damage control measures she could have been saved ... but that's another story!

At the outbreak of war in September 1939, the Royal Navy had just six aircraft carriers; Ark Royal – new and purpose-built (72 aircraft, 30 knots), Glorious, Furious and Courageous – all converted from light battlecruisers 1925-1930 (36-48 aircraft, 30 knots), Eagle – converted 1924 (21 aircraft, 24 knots) and Hermes – converted 1924 (12 aircraft, 25 knots). Within the first nine months of war, by June 1940, both Glorious and Courageous had been lost.

Then in November 1941, Ark Royal, the pride of the fleet was also lost! Fortunately, by that time two new carriers, Illustrious and Formidable, had joined the fleet. These were much more heavily armoured, after the experience of Courageous and Glorious, and were to be followed later by Implacable, Indefatigable, Indomitable and Victorious.

Fred Thornton

FRED Thornton of Birkenhead was a boy seaman on board the giant aircraft carrier HMS Glorious when she was sunk in those Arctic waters. He was one of only 41 survivors out of over 900 who had taken to the lifeboats, some subsequently spending four days in the water.

After rescue by Norwegian trawlers they were taken to the Faroe Islands where, sadly, a few were to die of their injuries.

The survivors, though, were later transferred to Scotland

Fred, left, with Jim O'Neill at their first reunion in 1968 in the Isle of Man.

Fred Thornton of Birkenhead, Gerry Salt (whose elder brother perished on Glorious, and who has done much of the research into the tragedy) and Bill Smith of Prenton at a recent reunion.

for further medical attention. However, Fred had been taken straight to Rosyth aboard a destroyer ahead of his shipmates as he was not in as poor condition as some of them who too unfit to travel.

Fred remembers vividly the time spent afterwards in the hospital in Edinburgh where all the survivors were eventually taken. "I was hopelessly spoiled because I was the youngest, still just a kid really. All the others made a great fuss of me and the Marchioness of Bute, who used to come and visit us all, always had a special treat for me, like strawberries from her garden."

Fred went back to sea again in the Royal Navy and after the war subsequently joined the merchant navy.

In 1968 Fred's sister was on holiday in Douglas on the Isle of Man when she spotted a picture of the HMS Glorious on the wall of the hotel. When she enquired of the licensee, James O'Neill, she discovered that he, too, was

one of the original 41 survivors. As a result of that chance sighting Fred went over to meet Jim who had been in the very next bed to him in the hospital in Edinburgh.

"It was quite a reunion as you can imagine," said Fred, "Very emotional after nearly thirty years to meet again a shipmate with whom you had shared so much."

Fred was to be surprised again, in 1975, when he learned that Bill Smith of Prenton, who then worked at Cammell Lairds, was also a survivor of the Glorious. They had each believed themselves to be the only 'local' survivor whilst living only a few miles apart.

They had not, however, known each other whilst on board Glorious, not surprising in a complement running to 1200 plus, and they did not meet when rescued as Fred had been taken on ahead to Scotland.

Today Fred is still cleaning windows in Prenton. *"Sometimes in the winter this job can be worse than floating in those Arctic waters. I think I've suffered more here than I ever did in all my years in the navy!"*

Fred's "Certificate for Wounds and Hurts" issued shortly after his hospitalisation.

W M

Working ships of the Mersey

M.V. Menestheus
by Les Cowle

BLUE Funnel Line's motor vessel "Menestheus", 8,510 gross registered tons, was built in 1958, the second of six sister ships, namely, "Menelaus", "Machaon", Memnon", "Melampus" and "Maron".

She was completed in 1958 for the then Ocean Steamship Company, and operated on the Liverpool to Far East trade, China and Japan, calling at Penang, Port Swettenham, Singapore and Hong Kong, etc, a route familiar to many who probably made these voyages regularly in "Blueys".

In this print from Les Cowle's original oil painting, she is depicted outward bound from Liverpool in the 1960's. In 1977 she was transferred to Ocean Group's Elder Dempsters, as, ultimately were most of her sisters, and she was renamed "Onitsha". Her life with Elder Dempsters, however, was short lived, and she was sold to Thenamaris Maritime Inc. of Piraeus, and became the "Elisland", registered in Cyprus. Sadly she was broken up in March 1979 at Kaohsiung - the end of yet another graceful Blue Funnel Ship.

Les Cowle

Marine Artist

Born in Birkenhead in the 1930s, Les Cowle went to Cathcart Street school before attending Birkenhead Institute in Whetstone Lane.

He served an apprenticeship to Marine Engineering with Alfred Holt & Co, joining the sea staff as an engineer in 1952. He remained at sea throughout the 50s subsequently serving with other well known Liverpool Shipping Companies as Brocklebanks, Ellerman Papayanni, Canadian Pacific, Hendersons and Bibby Line.

Now retired after a varied career in the paper industry, he latterly returned to shipping with Ocean Fleets Ltd, and worked for a while as a Consultant Marine Engineer. He is a fellow of the Institute of Marine Engineers.

Les lives with his wife, a retired nursing sister, in Bebington, and they have two grown up sons. He keeps very busy painting ships for pleasure, and also, when invited, to commission. His paintings are quite well known, and some of them hang in the offices of companies both here and overseas.

His paintings are frequently used as company Christmas cards, and also by the Blue Funnel Association, of which he is a member.

Kingsmead School, Meols, Hoylake

Principal
ARTHUR T. WATTS
M.A.(Camb). B.Sc (London)
Late scholar of Peterhouse, Cambridge, and
24th Wrangler.
Assisted by
J. HENRY WATTS, M.A.
Late Exhibitioner Kings College, Cambridge
———— **and others.** ————

THE School is situated in its own grounds in Bertram Drive, and is a few minutes walk from the sea. The position is very open, commanding a view of the Cheshire and Welsh Hills. A large playing field is attached to the School.

Boys are prepared for the Universities, Professions or Business.

The Examinations taken are the London and Liverpool University Matrics, and the Cambridge Locals. The Religious teaching is thoroughly Evangelical, and is based on the full inspiration of the Bible.

*Preparatory Department
for Boys under 8*
Prospectus for Boarders and Day Boys
on application

Registered Charity Nº 525920

KINGSMEAD SCHOOL
Founded in 1904 ... *Going from Strength to Strength*

Wirral's only boarding and day school

Teaching children from 3 - 16 with a
separate Kindergarten for 2 year olds

Preparation for 11+, 13+ to senior
independent schools, and GCSE

Flexible boarding in a family setting

*For more information contact the Headmaster
Mr E.H. Bradby, MA (Oxon)*

**Bertram Drive, Hoylake
Wirral L47 0LL
Telephone: 0151 632 3156
Facsimile: 0151 632 0302**

CAMMELL LAIRD
& CO LTD
BIRKENHEAD

SHIPBUILDERS
BOILERMAKERS

ENGINEERS
REPAIRERS

LONDON: 3, CENTRAL BUILDINGS, WESTMINSTER, S.W.I.

The Island

by Win Moreland

We remember childhood summers
When the sun shone every day.
How we walked out to the Island,
And played pirates in a cave.

We knew all about the spring tides,
And all about the neaps.
How long we could stay there,
And when the tide would turn.

Which way lay the sinking sand,
Which way lay the mud
That sucked the sandals off our feet,
And oozed between our toes.

Who taught us how to cross the sands,
To understand the tides,
To recognise a cormorant,
And know a curlew's cry?

We can't remember who they were,
But now we find ourselves,
Telling children wearing trainers
The way to cross the sands.

They will remember summers
When the sun shone every day.
How they walked out to the Island
And played pirates in a cave.

Storeton Village and 'Avenues'

Storeton Hall - the remains of the Great Chamber with the Solar above - all that is left today

> **Storeton, or indeed, 'Stourton' as it was originally known, was a place of much more importance than its present tranquillity would indicate**

THE village of Storeton is one of those quaint little backwaters of Wirral which you may pass through on your way somewhere else. In some ways it is hard to appreciate it as a 'village' at all.

It doesn't have a church or a pub, or even any shops, although it did once have a school. Simply, it doesn't fit in with one's usual concept of a 'village'. But quite a few people live there and they would be rightly offended if they were to read such allegations.

However, in much earlier times Storeton, or indeed,

'Stourton' as it was originally known, was a place of much more importance than its present tranquillity would indicate. In many ways it can be considered as a focal point or 'hub' of old bye-ways which criss-crossed Wirral. One such example is the old "Roman Road" from Woodchurch, through Prenton and into the village itself. Whether it ever felt the feet of Roman soldiers two thousand years ago is somewhat doubtful, but it certainly would have been a route used by monks in the middle ages. Thus, it is also referred to as "The Monk's Steps".

The pathway, which is quite probably medieval in origin, is paved in places with large well-worn flat slabs of stone almost like stepping-stones as it crosses the low lying boggy fields to Prenton.

The Roman connection may well have been acquired by this pathway because of the inscribed and carved Roman Stones, presently in the Grosvenor Museum in Chester, which very likely came from the nearby Storeton Hill quarries, which were worked even in early Roman times. More recently twentieth century 'Lords and Landowners', notably William Hesketh Lever, altered much of the original topography of this area.

On Thursday 28th September 1911, at an auction held in the Woodside Hotel by Boult Son & Maples, William Hesketh Lever bought all 64 lots comprising an estate of

Storeton school, built by Brocklebank in 1865, sold to Lever in 1911, is now a private house having been recently renovated.

The formal gatehouse at Thornton Manor

1,538 acres, off the Trustees of the estate of the late Sir Thomas Brocklebank. This included, seven large farms, a quarry, a private railway, numerous cottages and smallholdings and "the entire parish of Storeton".

With his earlier huge land purchases, including Brimstage in 1908, he then set about reorganising the landscape of central Wirral to suit his own grand ideas of planning and architecture. His country seat at Thornton Manor had been totally rebuilt to become the new 'focal point' for the roads and bye-ways of Wirral. (Though the word bye-ways was something of a misnomer.)

Gracious avenues of trees marched in straight lines across the Wirral landscape, to his order, almost in the manner of the Romans 2,000 years previously. Storeton,

> ... this included, seven large farms, a quarry, a private railway, numerous cottages and smallholdings and "the entire parish of Storeton"

Right: The end of the main avenue which would bring Lever to his gatehouse (pictured top left)

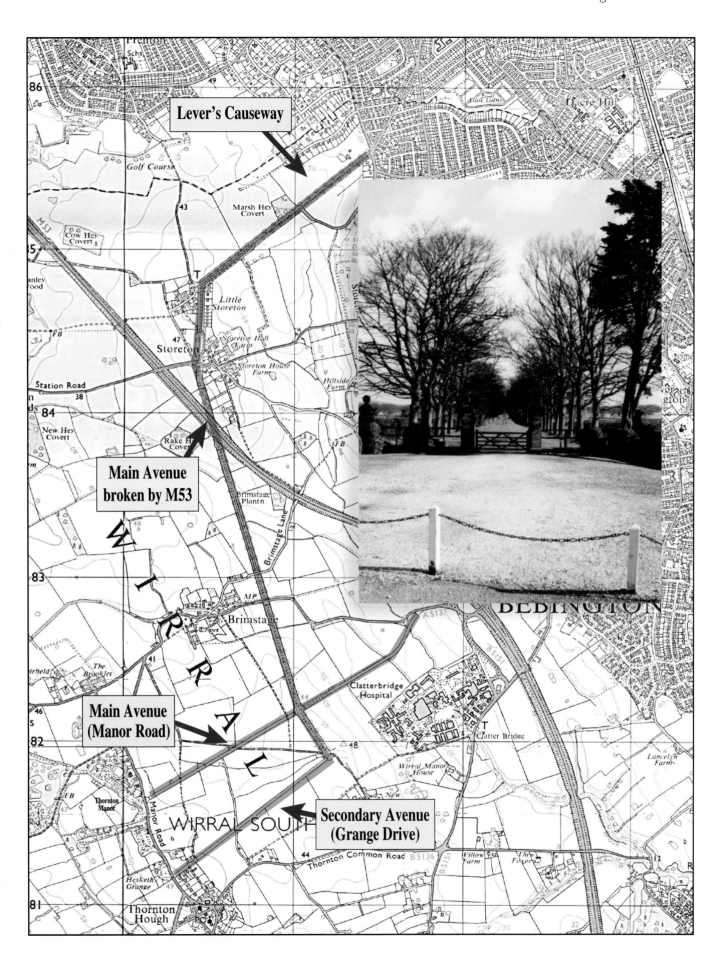

Lever's Causeway

Main Avenue
broken by M53

Main Avenue
(Manor Road)

Secondary Avenue
(Grange Drive)

"Gracious avenues of trees marched in straight lines across the Wirral landscape"

Thornton Manor, the Lever family home and focus of the 'avenues' of Wirral, had been totally rebuilt.

itself, was changed by the 'Lever Causeway' which came down from Mount Road like a modern day motorway, into the village, obliterating the old gently meandering Marsh Lane.

Then it changed direction sharply, went straight through the back of the old village and across the fields towards Thornton Hough. William Hesketh Lever was no respecter of tradition, or landscape, or village life, he didn't need to be, after all it was HIS village!

He changed for ever this little backwater. It was to become little more than a 'gatehouse' to his grand avenue. The avenue itself 'carved' its way across the farmland of his newly acquired estates, across Brimstage Lane, across Brimstage Road, and on to a point just west of Clatterbridge where it met

two other 'Lever' avenues, coming from Brackenwood and Thornton Common, before turning south west to finish at Thornton Manor itself. From whatever direction he approached his 'home' he could do so on his own private roads!

He even constructed a 'secondary avenue' which led on to the house he built nearby for his father, Hesketh Grange.

Ironically, this grand avenue was, in turn, 'carved up' by our own 'latter day Philistines', the motorway engineers, whose M53, running deep in a cutting, severed Lever's avenue just south of Storeton. Thankfully, the 'grand old man' was not here to see it!

However, to return almost 1,000 years....

After the Norman conquest of the late eleventh century, and the subsequent compilation of the Domesday Book, Storeton formed part of the estates of Nigel de Burci who was a retainer of the Baron of Halton. Some time later, around 1120, the Storeton lands, together with Puddington and the 'Forest of Wirral', were presented by the Earl of Chester to his steward, Alan Sylvester, the 'Forester of Wirral'. It was the same Alan Sylvester who was the owner of the original "Wirral Horn" which has come to be used to this day as an emblem of the peninsula.

Storeton Hall was, at that time, the home of the Sylvesters. A century later, Alan's great-grand-daughter, Agnes, married Sir Thomas Bamville and the Hall passed into their ownership until, again through the female line, their eldest daughter married Sir William Stanley. The Stanleys then held the Hall for six centuries until 1848, when it was bought by the Brocklebank shipping family!

Much of the Hall dated from the mid-fourteenth century, but it may not have been the principal residence of the Stanleys for all that time. Indeed, in the late fifteenth century, another Sir William Stanley built Hooton Hall, an altogether grander place. The Stanleys were to become one of the most influential families in the north. His second son, Sir John Stanley, became Lord Deputy of Ireland, married Isabella, heiress of Lathom, and founded the dynasties of the Earl of Derby and Lord Stanley of Alderley.

But back to the Hall. Today little remains other than part of the main chamber which is incorporated into farm buildings at Storeton Hall Farm. Sad to think what could now have existed at Storeton if a family were to have stayed on at the Hall to this day. Over the last 150 years through the stewardship of the Brocklebanks and the Levers, the hall has been neglected whilst they turned their attentions to grander plans elsewhere.

> Ironically, this grand avenue was, in turn, 'carved up' by our own 'latter day Philistines', the motorway engineers, whose M53, running deep in a cutting, severed Lever's avenue just south of Storeton

Dreams

by

Cyrus Ferguson

That's all it was, just another dream.
Like all the dreams before it, without foundation.
Without reality, all we have are thoughts and dreams.
But reality is truth, and not to compare with dreams.
When dreams and truth coincide, happiness must surely follow.
But seldom they go hand in hand and so I dream until tomorrow.

To inspire a dream, you have a quality, someone wants to share.
But dreams cannot be shared, they must be lived, then forever lost.
And so my love I dream of you, today, tomorrow, and evermore.
Knowing in my heart that my dream, in reality, can never really be.
That is no fault of you my love, and never could it be.
The reality of my dream is the pleasure of knowing you,
Of loving you from afar, and in my dreams you love me too.

If the reality of my dreams is that I have loved, and lost,
Then I think that it is better to have lived the dream than not.
At least I have the memories, and the chance to dream again.
And so I dream once more, and in my dream, the reality is lost.
But if I had only one last wish my love,
The reality would my dream come true.
And so, I dream, and dream again, my love
And in each dream, reality is you.

The 13th (Service) Battalion Cheshire Regiment

The 13th (Service) Battalion Cheshire Regiment embodied all the traditions that personified a 'Pals' battalion.

BY SEPTEMBER 1914 the country was gripped by a fervour the likes of which will probably never be seen again. The need for young men to get at the enemy before it was all "over by Christmas" seems almost perverse today.

A sign of the times no doubt, but, who were these blood-thirsty men? What was in their background that made them this way? The answers are many and varied. They were the flower of British youth (it can be argued that they were the flower of the world's youth of the day). They were the children and grandchildren of the Victorian Empire. They could not let those childhood stories of war against the enemies of the Empire go unanswered. And, as mentioned earlier, it was due to be all over by Christmas, so they didn't want to miss out.

In the early days of the First World War it became apparent to some at the top that the expected rout of the German Army was not going according to plan. Our small army was being slaughtered, there was a need to get more men, and fast. The Territorial Army was the next to go into action, though the terms of their recruitment before the war meant they did not have to serve abroad. Fortunately, there were some of our leaders, both political and industrial, who were forward looking enough to try and do something about this situation.

As early as August 1914 Kitchener made his appeal for '100,000 men', the hope being that the county regiments would each raise a new Battalion. The length of service for these men being the duration of the war, the battalions were called 'Service' battalions. Around this time the 17th Earl of Derby is given credit for the idea of forming 'Pals' battalions, these being formed of men who were related, who worked together, were in the same football team etc. The success of this idea was as astonishing as it was disastrous, but, this disaster would not befall the Pals for some time. Uniquely the Pals were the men who were the mid and junior management of the industrial cities and towns of the North.

The 13th (Service) Battalion

Cheshire Regiment was one of them. They embodied all the traditions that personified a 'Pals' battalion. Essentially coming from two main areas on the Wirral peninsula. The first group was raised by the MP Mr Gershom Stewart, and consisted of approximately 500 men from Wallasey, New Brighton, Seacombe and Liscard area.

Intended to join the Liverpool

Pals, they were taken to Liverpool by Mr Stewart, but, recruitment was so fast that the authorities stopped recruiting to allow time to catch up with the paper work. Mr Stewart brought his men back to Wirral.

He later met up with William Hesketh Lever, of Lever Brothers, who by the end of the war was to 'contribute' nearly 4,000 men and women from all parts of the world to the war effort (!). The second group was raised by Lever at Gladstone Hall in Port Sunlight Village and consisted of approximately 700 men, the majority of whom worked at Lever Brothers, or were the sons, brothers or relatives of Port Sunlight residents.

There were also groups from Ellesmere Port, Hoylake, West Kirby, Chester and Liverpool.

On 7th September 1914 the Battalion was marched to Chester Castle with Mr Stewart and Mr Lever at the head and put under the command of Captain Field. After arriving at Tidworth Camp on Salisbury Plain several NCOs from the Guards were waiting to get them into shape. During a year long period of training they moved to Codford, Bournemouth and finally to Aldershot. Subsequently, as part of the 25th Division, they left for France on 25th September 1915. They fought

Lever's young men of Port Sunlight, accompanied by the Port Sunlight Silver Band, marching off to Chester to enlist in the 'Pals' in 1914

Fortunately, there were some of our leaders, both political and industrial, who were forward looking enough to try and do something about this situation.

Wirral Memories

in France during the battle of the Somme, they fought in Belgium during the battle for the Messines Ridge and at Ypres.

The casualty list up to December 1917 showed that 28 officers had been killed with 68 wounded, and 293 other ranks killed with 1,458 wounded. To this figure can be added approximately 420, of all ranks, missing. A high price to pay in just 2 years and 3 months. These figures do not take account of the men who left the battalion having taken up commissions and promotions.

By February 1918 the condition of the men remaining in the battalion being so poor, the decision was taken to disband them and disperse them amongst the other battalions of the division and some among other battalions of the Regiment. The casualty toll of men from the 13th will thus be much greater when account is taken of later casualties with these other battalions.

The men who died have been relatively easy to find out about, their details being recorded by many official bodies, the Commonwealth War Graves Commission, war grave registers, local community memorials and some family members. It has been without doubt hardest of all, though, to find any information on the men who survived.

This said, some survived a

shadow of the man who joined up, with ill health caused by the terrible privations suffered by all and gas poisoning suffered by many. What is now called shell-shock, a thing barely accepted by the military and medical authorities at the time, being suffered by many apparently healthy young men. We can say, though, that of this group, one went on to be Britain's oldest living person, Mr Bill Proctor. One went on to father 11 children, Mr Arthur Onions. All returned to 'civvies' and made the best of what they had.

Our intention is to write a book on this battalion to show how they played their part in the Great War and the effect it, and they, had on Lever Brothers and Port Sunlight and, indeed, on Wirral itself. Our main problem has been, and still is, the lack of photographs and personal details. Given that the war ended some 80 years ago, the surviving relatives are, in the main, grandchildren, many of whom don't even know if grandfather was in the war anyway. We should point out that the surviving children of these men have, in the main, been very helpful to us, nearly all having photographs or documents for us to copy.

Lastly, though, the officers have been a great problem. In the main they did not come from Wirral or, indeed, from what is now Merseyside. They came from Sussex, Kent, Oxfordshire, etc.

Capt. E.C.W. Arend. An officer with the 13th of which absolutely nothing is known. Can anyone cast any light on this gentleman?

Pictures and documents relating to this important group of men are scarce, this said though, they must exist. The families of these officers and men must have wondered what their relatives did in the war. W M

A view from Central Station

by John Lindsey

The King Edward VII Memorial Clock in 1938 — back where it used to be, but before the advent of the tunnel flyovers. In the 20s it had been moved fifty yards east — John Lindsey never knew why.

AS soon as I walked out of Central Station it hit me. A great tidal wave of nostalgia. It was over thirty years since I last stood on this spot but I would not mind having a pound for every moment spent there in the previous thirty years, waiting for a bus or, in the old days, a tram.

I was born in Higher Tranmere, in a house which is now a pet food shop. No plaque commemorates its illustrious history! There were no buses then. The Woodside – Victoria route was served by 4-wheel trams on which both ends of the top deck were open to the elements. Even when the very grand 8-wheelers, completely enclosed (over in Liverpool they called them "green goddesses") were introduced Tranmere did not enjoy this improvement. The gradient was probably too steep or the curves too sharp for these monsters.

Certainly my maternal grandmother thought so. She lived in North Wales and when she came to visit us she would take a tram from Woodside station but always got off when it reached Central station. She would then walk to the top of the hill. She was convinced that to continue her journey up Argyle Street South on the tram was far too risky.

In the early twenties we moved to Prenton, not far from Tranmere Rovers' ground. I have vivid recollections of sitting at the front window on a Saturday

Argyle Street South, which was considered "far too steep and dangerous" by John Lindsey's Welsh grandma on visits to Tranmere — she would get off the tram and walk up the hill!

afternoon, watching supporters streaming along Borough Road, with tram drivers continually clanging their bells to clear a path through the crowds which stretched from pavement to pavement. In the early years of the club my father bought shares which were handed down to me. I'm not the only one who wishes that attendances today were as large as they were in those far off days.

I remember watching Dixie Dean and Pongo Waring when they were showing the first signs of exceptional talent which led them eventually to international fame, and I was one of the excited fans raising the roof when the Rovers ran in thirteen goals against, I think, Oldham.

One of my abiding memories of Prenton Park, however, is concerned not with the interior of the ground but the open fields which then stood on the other side of Borough Road. With three or four chums I had gone for a walk, probably to Victoria Park, and on the way back one bold spirit suggested we should chase some sows grazing in the meadow alongside Prenton Road East. The idea did not appeal to me all that much but my fear of cows was not as strong as my fear of being thought a coward so I joined in.

Such was our excitement that we failed to notice the approach of an irate herdsman. We fled in all directions and only one was caught. I was swept up under one arm and as we made off towards the farmhouse I pleaded with him to let me go. My entreaties seemed to fall on deaf ears so I offered the ultimate bribe, "You can come to our house for tea."

Whether this invitation was irresistible or he was merely adjusting his grip I don't know but I wriggled free and set off for home as fast as my little legs would carry me. I became aware that he was in hot pursuit but with the aid of wings lent by fear I made it with a few yards to spare. When he arrived at the back door I hid behind my mother's skirts. "Here you are m'am", he said, "I've brought the lad's shoe. He left it behind."

He did not stay for tea.

The view from Central Station has changed dramatically since I was last there. The King Edward VII Memorial Clock tower is back where it used to be. About seventy years ago it was moved about fifty yards to the east; I never knew why. Then again I gather it had to move to make way for the eyesore of the tunnel flyover.

Some landmarks have gone. The swimming baths opposite the side entrance to the station, for example. And Birkenhead Town station is no longer there. I don't think that in all the years when I passed that way I ever saw a soul either entering or leaving that station. I used to wonder why it was there.

Outside the gas works, around the corner from Central station, there used to be an open space. Workers held meetings there when they were on, or thinking of going on, strike. On one occasion a picture in the paper carried a caption saying it showed strikers. As a prominent figure in the foreground was this humble reporter I complained to the editor that it was a defamation of character.

The Central Hotel is still there hiding behind the flyover and the clock. I remember it being opened; in fact I produced the pictorial supplement which the "News" published to mark the occasion. As a measure of its attractions prominence was given to the fact that one of its first residents was Elizabeth Welsh, "star of stage, screen and radio", who was appearing at the nearby Argyle Theatre.

WM

Below: The Argyle Theatre, here in the 20s, remained virtually unaltered till Hitler took a hand on 21st September 1940, when it received a direct hit from an incendiary bomb and was burned out. The site now forms Beatties car park.

Above: One of the old 4-wheel part-open trams used on the Tranmere route, (T), in the 20s and 30s. Originally fully open the closed section was added to most of them before the first war, the remainder were completed in 1922.

Sand in my Shoes

by Richard Hutson

High fashion on the beach at Hoylake in 1929.

Author Richard Hutson recalls his childhood in Hoylake after the first war

IN 1922, soon after the Great War ended, my parents brought me to live in Hoylake.

I was four years old, too young to appreciate what an exciting playground was to be mine. Range upon range of sand dunes stretched from the "elementary" school in Hoyle Road to Meols, and from the promenade to the main Birkenhead Road. The sand was only interrupted by Monkey Wood, a copse of pine trees where, aged six, I escaped from my mother and was nearly murdered by a young woman who took my hand, led me into the dark wood and beat me about the head with a tree branch.

Later that day my horrified parents with their much subdued and bandaged offspring, accompanied by a policeman, confronted the lunatic in her kitchen where,

"The sand was everywhere. Like Bedouins encamped in the Sahara Desert we were besieged by it ... "

armed with a carving knife, she stood at bay.

Mother and I retreated hastily and I suppose this incident should have taught me to mistrust persuasive young women who invite one to walk in the woods – but I cannot recall that it did!

The sand was everywhere. Like Bedouins encamped in the Sahara Desert we were besieged by it. Sand filled our shoes, our hair, our clothes. From there it was carried into the house where gritty particles even reached the beds and penetrated between the sheets.

Sandheys slipway to the left and Monkey Wood in the centre, scene of Richard's 'narrow escape', were features of the front at Hoylake in 1920s.

When gale winds blew, the sand swirled around us like miniature tornadoes, twisting and writhing to pile up against the garden fences and to lie in golden banks along the promenade. We cleared sand as others cleared snow.

In the 20s Hoylake expanded rapidly from a quiet fishing village to a dormitory town for commuters from Liverpool. The steam train from 'town' carried office workers during the week and 'trippers' at week-ends.

New houses began to invade the sandhills and new shops appeared in Market Street.

The installation of a telephone in our home, an instrument not then in general use, enabled my mother to shop without leaving the house.

This was an unheard-of luxury made possible by the cheerful errand boys who brought the goods on bicycles. Each bike would bear the name of the tradesman on a metal plate fixed under the cross-bar.

Most of our fish was bought from the flat-topped handcarts of the hawkers who assembled daily at the Sandheys slipway to meet the boats. Sand dabs and plaice in summer with an occasional wing of ray or a river sole, the local name for a Dover sole. In winter codling, whiting and shrimps, boiled on board the boats, sold by the pint still steaming hot.

Despite our healthy outdoor life many more infections were commonly caught than children suffer today. No modern child need fear scarlet fever, diphtheria or polio-myelitis.

Each winter measles, whooping cough, chicken pox and mumps were as regular as influenza. Wirral had at least one fever hospital. Hoylake was probably healthier than most towns but growing up in the 20s was still a dangerous process ...

Richard Hutson

about the author ...

RICHARD HUTSON joined the cadet training ship HMS Conway in 1934 when it was moored off Rock Ferry in the Mersey.

He subsequently became Chief Cadet Captain and was awarded the King's Gold Medal. After two years training he went to sea as a midshipman with the Blue Funnel Line of Liverpool trading with the Far East, Australia and North America.

He completed his apprenticeship and on the outbreak of war in 1939 he transferred to the Royal Navy. He continued to serve at sea throughout the war

It is a tale of adventure,
of modern day swashbucklers ...

specialising in navigation and holding the rank of Lieutenant (N*)RNR.

After the war Richard attended the University of Sheffield and in 1950 was awarded a Bachelor of Arts degree with special honours in Geography. Shortly afterwards he was invited to return to the Blue Funnel Line and take responsibility for cadet training.

As principal of Ocean Fleets Training Establishment in Liverpool he trained many hundreds of young men and women for the sea services of Britain and for the developing countries in the Far East.

Originally a native of Hoylake, and an old boy of Calday Grange Grammar School, Richard, a widower of many years, now lives in retirement in Anglesey. His

interests are gardening, natural history and working in his local village community, but his passion is writing!

He has written several books and his latest, "The Nine Lives of Ding Dong Bell", is based on his 25 years experiences at sea before, during and after the war.

It is a story told as fiction through the imaginary character of Captain John Bell and describes the true adventures of the author himself. The setting is world-wide, spanning every ocean and all latitudes from the Arctic to the Coral Sea.

He describes the carriage of pilgrims to Mecca, the search for opium in Columbia and voyaging to China before the communist revolution as a deck officer's apprentice.

This is how the maritime world existed half a century ago and this is how, in peace and war, in warships and merchant vessels, the seamen of Britain served their country.

It contains many references to his early days in Hoylake and the Wirral and his contact with the fishing fleets of the 1930's.

It is a tale of adventure, modern day swashbucklers, and yet also an historical account, even a documentary. It is a look into the recent past which to some is still a memory but to most will be a fascinating historical insight.

The book is printed in Beaumaris, close to his home. It is A5 size & 140 pages with photographs, line drawings and woodcuts. Priced £8.95 – inc post & packing.

You can order direct from the author. Telephone 01248 490 376

Local Heroes

Cyril Gourley, V.C

Our picture of Cyril Gourley is, in itself, of interest, because according to Army records, Cyril was commissioned by the time he received his decoration, but the photograph (taken by G. Watmough Webster of West Kirby) clearly shows him in sergeant's uniform wearing the medal ribbon, and indeed it has been signed on the back with his name and "V.C."

CYRIL was born on 19th January 1893 and lived at 23 North Road, West Kirby. He was educated at Calday Grange Grammar School where he distinguished himself by winning the Edward Rathbone Scholarship, and went on to Liverpool University.

In 1913 he became the first student to take the final examination for the new degree of Bachelor of Commercial Science, gaining distinctions in Economics, French and Commerce.

On leaving University he joined Alfred Holt & Co. Ltd. At the outbreak of war in 1914, he joined the Territorial Army in the 4th West Lancashire Howitzer Brigade, of the Royal Field Artillery.

The Brigade was mobilised on 4th August 1914, and on 28th September 1915, they embarked for France sailing in two ships with their horses and guns and other equipment. One ship belonged to the Elder Dempster Line and the other was the I.O.M. steamer Mona's Queen. They moved into the line in the Kemmel area south of Ypres as part of the 55th West Lancs Division.

On 20th July 1916, they moved to positions on the Somme and were located in the area of the dreaded village of Guillemont, the scene of so much bitter fighting and bloodshed. Although there were only minor skirmishes of infantry patrols throughout much of the winter the artillery were often subjected to enemy barrages.

On the lst June 1917, they became part of the massed 2,233 pieces of artillery that rained shells on the enemy for seven days almost continuously for the attack on Messines Ridge.

An enemy shell set fire to the camouflage putting the whole of the ammunition dump at serious risk. Sergeant Gourley's prompt action in extinguishing the blaze saved the situation, and for this he was awarded the Military Medal.

In the third week of November they moved to take part in the first Battle of Cambrai, the 7th Battery taking position close to the

> **He did not marry, and was to die peacefully in his sleep in 1982 at the age of 89 years. His body was brought back to West Kirby to be buried with his parents in Grange Cemetery**

Lempire Road at Little Priel Farm. They had opened fire on 30th November 1917 at around 7 a.m and after about half an hour found themselves under attack from enemy artillery with the result that a section officer was seriously wounded.

The Battery commander, Major J. Hudson M.C., had no other officer available and sent down Sergeant Gourley to take charge. The enemy maintained their barrage and their massed infantry were moving in close to the forward positions, in an attempt to breach the lines. All but one of the guns were knocked out of action.

The citation in the London Gazette of 13th February 1918, stated - "*For most conspicuous bravery when in command of a section of howitzers.*"

Though the enemy advanced in force, getting within 400 yards, Sgt. Gourley managed to keep one gun in action practically throughout the whole day. Though frequently driven off he always returned carrying ammunition, laying and firing the gun himself, taking first one and then another of the detachment to assist him.

When the enemy approached he pulled his gun out of the pit and engaged a machine gun at 500 yards, knocking it out with a direct hit. All day he held the enemy in check, firing with open sights on enemy troops in full view at 300 to 800 yards, and thereby saved his guns, enabling them to be withdrawn at nightfall. He was awarded the Victoria Cross for his actions that day.

On 5th January 1918, he was commissioned as a Second Lieutenant in the Royal Field Artillery. He was to remain with the now famous 55th Division until it was disbanded in 1919. He was appointed Acting Captain on 19th May 1919, and came home in June of that year to be demobilised.

On leaving the Army he joined Lever Brothers in the export department then known as the Marketing Advisory Service. He applied himself to his work with the same dedication he had displayed as a soldier, and it was largely due to his own efforts that the markets for the many Lever products were developed in the Balkans, Central and South America, and the Mediterranean countries.

He was a very quiet, courteous gentleman who, although always ready to help other people, shunned the adulation his great honour deserved. He continued to work until his retirement in 1958, having moved south in 1952 to Grayswood, near Haslemere, in Surrey where he lived with his mother and sister. For the next twenty four years he assumed a life of modest activity restoring his beautiful home and gardens, and keeping an interest in the associated farmlands.

He did not marry, and was to die peacefully in his sleep in 1982 at the age of 89 years. His body was brought back to West Kirby to be buried with his parents in Grange Cemetery.

After he was awarded the V.C., the 'C. E. Gourley V.C. Endowment' was founded in his honour, by a Trust deed dated 30th September 1919, by a committee appointed by the Hoylake and West Kirby Urban District Council. A sum of £1,500 was subscribed to provide a scholarship of £30 per year to Liverpool University.

The firm founded by his father and uncle - Gourley

When King George V and Queen Mary were in Liverpool on Saturday 19th July 1924 for the consecration of the new cathedral, Cyril Gourley was introduced to them.

Bros. still exists as a family firm on Merseyside.

It is thought that his father originated from Ireland, and in 1889 went to live in Liverpool until 1899 when they crossed the Mersey to live at 23 North Road, West Kirby.

In 1901, they moved to 39 Westbourne Road, West Kirby, continuing there until 1925 when they moved to 'Hill Close', School Lane, off Column Road, Grange, West Kirby. This later was to be known as 'Gourley's Grange', Gourley's Lane, in honour of Cyril E. Gourley V.C., M.M.

In the Second World War, Cyril Gourley, like so many other civilians, did his bit on duty as a 'Fire-watcher' during the many air raids.

In the Liverpool Echo of 6th March 1918, there is a report which sums up the modest character of this gallant man. Under the Headline 'Bashful Hero' it goes on ...

"The V.C. who 'stuck to his guns' all day and kept the Germans at bay almost unaided, had an attack of nerves when he met his colleagues at the Liverpool University.

Sergeant Cyril Gourley V.C., M.M., had a particularly cordial reception today. Some hundreds of students were in the liveliest form, and the echoing cheers and a noisy rattle, if they had been pitched in a lower key, would have resembled an 'artillery' demonstration.

Vice-Chancellor Dale, congratulated the modest hero on the honour he had gained, and mentioned that five V.C.s had now been won by old graduates and undergraduates of the University. Shaking hands with his parents and sister, who were witnesses of the interesting scene, he also tendered his heartiest congratulations to them.

Sergeant Gourley, flushed and bashful, drew the line at making a speech. In comparison with that the ordeal of battle was a triviality. So the Vice-Chancellor pleaded that time was precious, let the students once more give vent to their feelings as only students can, and hastened away with him to see the Lord Mayor."

On Saturday 19th July 1924, King George V accompanied by Queen Mary was in Liverpool for the consecration of the Cathedral. In the afternoon the King reviewed the 55th West Lancs. Territorial Division at the Wavertree Playground. Cyril Gourley V.C. was one of the nine V.C.s present at the time and spoke to His Majesty.

We are indebted to Denis Rose for this article & photograph